Class, Bureaucracy, and Schools

Class,
Bureaucracy,
and Schools

The Illusion of Educational
Change in America

Expanded Edition

MICHAEL B. KATZ

PRAEGER PUBLISHERS
New York

Published in the United States of America in 1975
by Praeger Publishers, Inc.
111 Fourth Avenue, New York, N.Y. 10003

This is the second, expanded edition of the book first published in 1971.

© 1971, 1975 by Praeger Publishers, Inc.

Library of Congress Cataloging in Publication Data

Katz, Michael B
  Class, bureaucracy, and schools

  (Praeger university series)
  Published in 1971 under title: Class, bureaucracy, and schools.
  Bibliography: p.
  Includes index.
  1. Education, Urban—United States—History.
2. Educational sociology—United States. 3. Educational—Aims and
objectives. I. Title.
LC5131.K36 1975   370.19′348′0973   74-9401
ISBN 0-275-52550-3
ISBN 0-275-85100-1 pbk.

Cover photograph by Betsy K. Frampton from Task Force on Children Out
of School, *The Way We Go to School: The Exclusion of Children in Boston*
(Boston: Beacon Press, 1971).

Printed in the United States of America

For Rebecca and Paul (1971)
and now Sarah (1974)

Contents

Preface to the First Edition

I shall begin this book with an excerpt from the most damning indictment of American education that I have yet encountered. It is the report of a task force on the exclusion of children from the Boston public schools, *The Way We Go to School* (Boston: Beacon Press, 1970). The report's power derives partly from the horrors it describes and, as well, from the traditional values it exemplifies. For, on the basis of this report, the Boston public school system stands condemned not only by romantics and radicals but also by the most long-standing and fundamental of American ideals.

Chapter VIII of the report describes the characteristics, attitudes, and role of attendance officers. This discussion provides a fitting introduction for what I have written in this book:

> Between September, 1968, and May, 1969, over 700 children were taken to court primarily due to their being truant from school. The attendance officer is instrumental in this court action: he acts as the prosecutor, gathering evidence against the child and presenting it in court. It is at the discretion of the officer whether to take a child to court.

When one member of the Task Force asked the Co-Head how he feels about taking children to court, he responded: ". . . we are often dissatisfied with the disposition because if a child gets off, others learn that going to court is not such a big thing. They don't fit the crime with the punishment anymore. That's the whole problem. . . ." Asked what kind of crime he was referring to, the Co-Head replied: "The crime of truancy."

Because of their dissatisfaction with court proceedings, the officers often use other methods in providing their services: "You've got to cajole or threaten. It becomes a question of forcing those wards [*sic*] to school. We tell the parents we'll take them to court or we'll stop their [pay] checks. It's not legal, of course, but we tell them that anyway."

The predisposition of the attendance officers to rely on court action and threats of court action stems, in part, from their backgrounds and training. The position of attendance officer is a civil-service one, with preference given to disabled veterans, veterans, and other people in that order. Aside from their military backgrounds, most of the officers have training in police work. Most of the forty-six officers now in the Department are former policemen.

In the course of our investigation we were told by a number of people, some within the School Department, that the position of attendance officer is a "political plum"—a highly paid, permanent position meted out on the basis of friendships and political connections. The salary, for example, is fixed at $15,400 per year, one of the highest paid positions within the School Department. (It is more than a teacher with a Ph.D. degree can make at the highest salary increment.) The annual Attendance Department budget for salary alone is . . . $741,000.

Recruitment procedures for the position are as questionable as are the officers' qualifications. The examination for the position is given sporadically. . . . A professional who works in a community agency reported to us that he has been attempting to take the examination since 1968. He has received no answer to his letters requesting the date of the next examination. When he goes in person to take the exam he is told that it was just given, or that there are no openings. Yet, he reports that new officers have been added to the Department several times during the period.

One School Department official told us that when there is a vacancy the position is filled immediately by a friend of an attendance officer or high-ranking school official, before interested citizens can compete for the opening. In support of this, he points out that none of the officers are black, Puerto Rican or Chinese, and that only four are women. . . . One of the Co-Heads . . . characterized all truant children as being "less intelligent, less well-scrubbed, crude, careless, and with pungent speech." Upon rebuttal of his statement, he responded: "Let's face it, these people are not school prone; they're just not. Their morals are certainly indicative of this."*

We often think of attitudes like these as characteristic of the nineteenth century. In fact, they are. One purpose of this book is to show the persistence of educational attitudes and structures in American cities over the past century and a quarter. Another is to proclaim and to account for the illusion of educational change in America.

* Pp. 57–60.

Preface to the Expanded Edition

In the fall of 1973 the publishers of *Class, Bureaucracy, and Schools* asked me whether I should like to prepare a revised edition. My answer was no; the book represents my point of view at a particular moment. It stands still; I hope my thinking doesn't. Indeed, although I do not disagree in any important way with the book's general conclusions, were I to write about the same subjects today, the result would be a different book. Thus, it is not possible to open up these chapters and tinker with their contents. They are like the school systems I describe: Only a thorough recasting would make any difference.

But, as I thought about the book, about its past reception and its future usefulness, I developed a rather different idea for a new edition. For the book has been remarkably successful in provoking intelligent discussion of the issues I hoped to raise, the nature of education, history, and reform. That discussion is perhaps its most important achievement. Consequently, it seemed to me in keeping with my intentions in writing this book to bring before readers some of the questions, comments, and criticisms it has provoked and at the same time to offer my own comments on the issues the book has raised and my own impressions of the way in which recent scholarship affects the arguments it proposes.

An epilogue to the book seemed an ideal way to add to its usefulness without the artificial process of revision. To begin the epilogue I originally chose the two essay reviews that struck me, not as the most laudatory, but as the most thoughtful. There, Marvin Lazarson and Carl Kaestle * raised questions that go beyond this book and others in its field to consider major issues in the study of history, education, and reform. However, considerations of length and cost have made it necessary to omit them. Nonetheless, I take up a number of the issues they raise in the essay that comprises the epilogue, first in a commentary on the most common criticisms of the book, then in a discussion of some of the most important and provocative recent scholarship on American education.

Fundamentally, I believe, dialogue is at the heart of scholarship, although, despite the professed ideals of academic life, it seldom takes place. Among people concerned with the history of education, there have been some hopeful signs in the last few years that a critical dialogue might emerge. I offer this expanded edition in the hope of advancing that development.

* Marvin Lazerson, "Revisionism and American Educational History," *Harvard Educational Review* 43 (May, 1973): 270–83, and Carl Kaestle, "Social Reform and the Urban School," *History of Education Quarterly* 12, No. 2 (Summer, 1972): 211–28.

Introduction

On a street corner in a Brooklyn slum there stands a modern school, a massive concrete block in the middle of an asphalt playground. Like an ancient fortress, it has long, narrow slits in place of windows. If I were a kid that building would frighten me. So would the windowless school that stands in Harlem. They remind me of the old schools in working-class neighborhoods of London, surrounded by high walls. Those walls testify that the first compulsory schools were alien institutions set in hostile territory. The same point could be made about contemporary educational fortresses in New York; one international feature of educational history that has remained intact is the separation of the school from the working-class community. Sometimes the outward appearance of a school has relevance to the activities that take place within it; that was so in those first compulsory schools in late-nineteenth-century England. It has often been so in New York; even the occasional capture of schools by progressives cannot change the assumptions that underlie their architectural design.

Consequently, there is logic in the choice of schools as objects of capture by communities seeking political and social emancipation. For the schools are fortresses in function as well as form, protected outposts of the city's educational establishment and the prosperous citizens who sustain it. In their own way, they are imperial institutions designed to civilize the natives; they exist to do something to poor children, especially, now, children who are black or brown. Their main purpose is to make these children orderly, industrious, law-abiding, and respectful of authority. Their literature and their spokesmen proclaim the schools to be symbols of opportunity, but their slitted or windowless walls say clearly what their history would reveal as well: They were designed to reflect and confirm the social structure that erected them.

There is a great gap between the pronouncement that education serves the people and the reality of what schools do to and for the children of the poor. Despite the existence of free, universal, and compulsory schooling, most poor children become poor adults. Schools are not great democratic engines for identifying talent and matching it with opportunity. The children of the affluent by and large take the best marks and the best jobs.

That fact cannot be explained either by genetics or by theories of cultural deprivation; it is the historical result of the combination of purpose and structure that has characterized American education for roughly the last hundred years. The purpose has been, basically, the inculcation of attitudes that reflect dominant social and industrial values; the structure has been bureaucracy. The result has been school systems that treat children as units to be processed into particular shapes and dropped into slots roughly congruent with the status of their parents. There is a functional relationship between the way in which schools are organized and what they are supposed to do. That relationship was there a century ago, and it exists today. This is why the issues of social class and bureaucracy are central to understanding the public school.

Purely contemporary analysis obscures this point. To appreciate the interweaving of structure and purpose in education it is necessary to study its origin and development. Today's educational structures are historical products; they represent patterns that have become deeply embedded in American society and are enormously resistant to change. The techniques with which the system maintains its equilibrium have themselves become traditions. We have become so accustomed to these ways of responding and to the assumptions enmeshed in existing structures that it is difficult to isolate and examine them clearly. But we gain detachment by looking at their origins. We can in fact pick out the moments when familiar features were new and controversial. We can analyze the interaction of social goals and social forces that entrenched those features in social history and ensured their survival over alternate proposals.

That is what this book attempts to do. Chapter 1 is schematic; it sets out to show the major organizational alternatives proposed for urban public education at a time when its structure was problematical. It makes the connection between social-class purposes, bureaucratic form, and the origins of urban school systems. By contrast, Chapter 2 is very concrete. Its purpose is to complement the essentially static analysis of organizational models with illustrations of educational development and an examination of the confrontation between bureaucracy and social reform.

This book concentrates on the years between 1800 and 1885; that was the critical period. My thesis is that by about 1880 American education had acquired its fundamental structural characteristics, and that they have not altered since. The final chapter considers that claim and the failure of subsequent reform movements which it implies. It considers the present moment in educational reform as well and concludes with a few concrete suggestions for reformers.

It may help the reader to understand the structure and details of this book if he knows something of its argument in advance. The central proposition that the book advances is, as I have said, that the basic structure of American education had been fixed by about 1880 and that it has not altered fundamentally since that time. The various parts are designed to demonstrate that point. They show how and why that structure came to be and, at less length, point out the continuities throughout the past century. If the central proposition is accepted, five important questions follow, and the book is designed to answer these, both implicitly and explicitly. First, did anyone propose alternatives to the structure that emerged? Second, was the establishment of that structure, regardless of alternative proposals, somehow "inevitable"? Third, what have been the interconnections between the major dimensions of that structure, or between its shape, its purpose, and its function? Fourth, why has the structure remained so resistant to reformist thrusts? And fifth, what is the moral of the structure's history for contemporary reform, or, must structural change precede "educational" change?

Acceptance of the proposition that the basic structure of American education has remained unchanged rests, quite obviously, on the definition of "basic." I mean by the term that certain characteristics of American education today were also characteristic nearly a century ago: it is, and was, universal, tax-supported, free, compulsory, bureaucratic, racist, and class-biased. Those features marked some educational systems by 1880; they diffused throughout the rest of the country in a sequence that roughly paralleled urban growth. In the first two chapters it will be apparent how education acquired these characteristics. In the last chapter I shall point out what is almost self-evident: that they persist today. I do not deny, or wish to imply that I deny, the introduction of important innovations—for instance, the kindergarten, vocational education, guidance, testing, and various new curricula, to name but a few. These have all made a difference, but they have not touched or altered the structural features I have outlined. It is to me, to use a very crude metaphor, as if the characteristics noted above form the walls of a box within which other sorts of change have taken place. The box is filled with objects that can be moved around and rearranged, but the walls themselves remain solid. Moreover, if I may extend the image for a moment, only objects that can fit within the box can be put there. Thus there is a congruence between the purposes and functioning of innovations that have entered the schools and the structural basis of the educational system itself.

This brief elaboration of my proposition should give meaning to the questions posed above. To take the first: Did anyone propose alternatives to the structure that emerged? Historians too often have conceived of educational history in simple moralistic terms: Good men—reformers of vision, dedication, and courage—proposed in embryo form the school system we now have. Opposing them were selfish, narrow-minded bigots interested in saving money and keeping the working classes down. We now know that this is nonsense, because we can see the consequences of those early proposals and because we find it hard today to accept simple, one-sided explanations of human behavior. But we must also reject the traditional story because of its constriction of historical vision. We must not accept the notion that there was but one educational proposal around which controversy revolved. On the contrary, in the first half of the nineteenth century four different proposals, four alternative modes of organizing public education, competed for acceptance. Each of them rested on a distinct and identifiable set of social values, and the competition among them reflected and expressed wider value conflicts within society, just as the Ocean Hill–Brownsville case or discussions of community control and decentralization do today. They were, additionally, real alternatives; examples of each did in fact exist. In Chapter 1 I shall present these models at length and the values on which they rested.

The second question is largely one of causation. The model that emerged victorious was the one I call incipient bureaucracy, and the question is, Why? Did bureaucracy triumph because it was somehow "inevitable"? It is a question of some importance for social theory as well as for historical inquiry. Perhaps naively, I see one implication to be that bureaucracy *is* inevitable. Given a complex, technological society and a complicated and massive social task like universal schooling, there is no other way of proceeding. Bureaucracy is neither good nor bad in this point of view; it is a social fact, a necessity. If we want schools, hospitals, welfare, or manufactured goods, we must have it, for the alternative is chaos and anarchy. If the logic of that point of view is accepted, then reform directed against the notion and existence of bureaucracy is at best romantic and, in any case, useless. It is better to accept the reality and permanency of bureaucracy and to improve its operation.

But if bureaucracy in education is inevitable, it did not seem so to some men who lived at the time of its creation. This is one moral of the story of alternative propositions. Some men at different points in time, in the nineteenth century and today, have been able to conceive of ways other than bureaucracy for managing the affairs of modern society. It is thus difficult to accept the proposition that bureaucracy is the only means through which social tasks can be accomplished.

In fact, on closer inspection, it appears that bureaucracy is inevitable only when men confront certain problems with particular social values and priorities. It is not industrialization that makes bureaucracy inevitable but the combination of industrialization and particular values. It is because of the mix of setting and priorities, not because of the setting alone, that we have bureaucracy as the dominant form of social organization. I shall return to this point in the last chapter, by which time the particular configuration of setting and priorities that produced bureaucracy should be clear.

My thesis about bureaucracy suggests an answer to the

third question I raised, concerning the interconnections between the dimensions of educational structure or, as we now might phrase it, between bureaucracy and social class. We know that education is bureaucratically organized; we know that it reflects class bias in its purposes and operations. Are the two features independent, at least in their origins if not in their present form? The answer is no. Bureaucracy came about because men confronted particular kinds of social problems with particular social purposes. Those purposes reflected class attitudes and class interests. Modern bureaucracy is a bourgeois invention; it represents a crystallization of bourgeois social attitudes. To its founders, as I hope the book will make clear, the purposes of the school system and its structure were clearly interrelated. They understood that part of the message they wished to have transmitted, the attitudes they wished formed, would inhere in the structural arrangements themselves rather than in explicit didactic procedures. What they did not admit, although it is hard to see how they could have failed to realize it, was that the bureaucratic structure, apparently so equitable and favorable to the poor, would in fact give differential advantage to the affluent and their children, thereby reinforcing rather than altering existing patterns of social structure. Through bureaucracy, the myth of equal opportunity has been fostered, while the amount of social mobility has been strictly regulated.

Once more we have clues to the answer to the next question: Why has the structure of American education remained impermeable to reformist thrusts? Part of the answer, of course, is that the structure serves powerful interests. It serves the interests of the educators by providing career-lines and regulating entry. They have no intention of permitting its alteration now, and they had none a century ago, as the example of Boston presented later in this book makes clear. The structures serve the interest of affluent groups, too, by working in favor of their children and giving them a disproportionate share of public funds. For those who control the system there has been no point in making fundamental structural alterations.

That is one reason the system has remained unreformed. Another is that very few people, until now, have seriously tried to change it. The reforms that have been proposed at various times, and frequently even enacted, generally consist of moving around the objects in the box, to return to my earlier image. I include in this description the reformers of the progressive period of the late nineteenth century, as I shall explain in the last chapter. Additionally, reformers have proceeded with an ineptitude of thought and strategy that has doomed their efforts from the very start. They have ignored the sociological constraints that impede changes within organizations and have lacked the strength or courage to think through the logic of their criticisms. Sometimes they have disturbed the equilibrium of a system for a few years, but in most cases it has reasserted itself, allowing things to continue pretty much in their old way. One clear instance of that was the abortive reform movement of the late 1870's in Boston, which is described in some detail in Chapter 2.

With the foregoing in mind, we can answer what to me seems a critical question confronting contemporary reformers: Must structural change precede educational change? Or is it possible to alter the purposes, biases, and actual functioning of schools without at the same time changing, radically, the structures through which they are organized and controlled? If my reading of history is roughly accurate, the answer to the second question is no. Forms of organizational structure are not and cannot be neutral. The relationships between bureaucracy, class bias, and racism are fixed. They emerged together a century ago, and they have remained essentially unchanged ever since. To attack one without the other would seem to be, if I am right, at best a waste of time and at worst another diversion from the serious need for social and educational reform within American society. Such is the message of this book.

Some will argue that this book is unduly presentist and that it twists the past in the service of contemporary positions on social issues. No historian can entirely divorce the categories with which he approaches the contemporary world from those with which he studies the past. Our concerns shape the questions that we ask and, as a consequence, determine what we select from the virtually unlimited supply of "facts." That state of affairs remains submerged and implicit in most historical work. In this case I have chosen to make manifest my questions and my concern. The concern is to provide a perspective that will be helpful in understanding and, I hope, improving urban education today.

Sociological concepts have been indispensable in forming that perspective, and I have used them deliberately and explicitly. The systematic use of concepts and the application of intellectual constructs give explanatory power to history, for they permit the formation of general statements. Too much historical work, however, continues to be remarkably unanalytical. It rests, for instance, on ideas about motivation that are quaint in terms of contemporary behavioral theory. It speaks of institutions and groups as if theories of society, organization, and stratification did not exist. As a consequence, written history usually offers no general statements that can be tested in different settings; it approaches data in a method so unsystematic that its findings cannot be replicated.

In short, there is little on-going, substantive discourse that permits historians to build on one another's work in any but the most primitive sense of adding more facts or extending the chronology backward or forward in time. It seems to me that the time for methodological unconsciousness within history has ended. Narrative history, uninformed by social or behavioral science, is pleasant and sometimes even interesting, but as a way of either advancing knowledge or contributing to substantive intellectual problems it is virtually useless.

Significant problems do not respect disciplinary boundaries; that is true for both intellectual and practical issues. Disciplines are constructs invented for the convenience of academics. They serve a useful function as a way of inducting new research workers into problems and providing an initial orientation to issues, but they should not be taken too seriously. The relations of structure and purpose in organizations, of bureaucracy and social class in education—these are not historical questions or sociological ones or some curious amalgam of the two. They are important intellectual problems that involve the past and the present, and they should be regarded in that light. Social science cut off from its historical base, as Robert Nisbet has elegantly demonstrated in *Social Change and History* (Oxford University Press, 1969), has weaknesses as grave as those of historical writing uninformed by social theory. The same can be said of social reform uninformed by history, which too often rests largely on myth. Myth, in turn, inhibits change by attaching sentimental or unreal value to institutions and forms that should be discarded.

History can serve reform partly by emancipating it from dependency upon an idealized past; it can help develop the strength of will and clear judgment that come from an ability to confront both past and present as they actually exist. That is a major purpose of this book. For we have many myths about education. We imagine educational arrangements that once were warm, democratic, and communal; we see the schools of long ago as providing a solid training in basic skills and opening up countless avenues of social mobility. We cast a rosy glow over the educational past and too often seek a restoration. But that image is a regressive fantasy and nothing more, as I hope this book will make clear.

Class, Bureaucracy, and Schools

1

Alternative Proposals for American Education: The Nineteenth Century*

There are no effective alternatives in American life. This is a realization to which the young came first and older reformers more slowly. The creation of a counterculture and the attempt to find alternatives to public schooling express the same impulse and the same truth. There is only one way to grow up in America if one wants to eat regularly, to be warm, and not to be harassed by the police. For the vast majority there is only one place to go to school, and that place is the same nearly everywhere. There is one city, one mode of production, one road to power. And there is little freedom. The essence of freedom resides in choice, and for most of us the range of

* A fully documented version of this chapter can be found in my article "From Voluntarism to Bureaucracy in American Education," *Sociology of Education*, Summer, 1971. This material is adapted and reprinted by permission of the American Sociological Association. Citations for quotations can be found in my *The Irony of Early School Reform: Educational Innovation in Mid-Nineteenth-Century Massachusetts* (Cambridge: Harvard University Press, 1968; reprinted by Beacon Press, 1970).

3

options in anything grows smaller. The uniformity shaped in the name of the public weal is a bankrupt social policy. It engenders a sense of overwhelming futility; there is no reason to work for change. Meanwhile, every serious social problem increases in scope and severity from year to year, and traditional approaches to social reform offer nothing very new.

This is why the search for alternative social policies has caught the imagination of workers in every field. It is the last hope. But although devising alternatives may be a nice intellectual game, creative and socially conscious, it can be no more than that—a fashionable and decadent exercise, a way of playing the fiddle while America burns. To go beyond that and inject realism into intellectual play is by no means easy. For there is a congruence between the rigid, centralist character of American life and its social and industrial structures. The weight of intellectual argument is, in fact, on the side of the proponents of inevitability, who argue that hard-headed acceptance of contemporary forms is the only way an advanced industrial society can manage its business, both public and private. That is the moral of functional social science.

It is a moral that many of us would rather not accept; to reject it, however, we must answer a very difficult question. Is it possible—in a fashion totally devoid of romantic posturing—to imagine a way in which things might be different, and a way in which that difference might be brought about? In the American past some people answered that question affirmatively. They did not answer it very well, for they failed, and they failed so completely that their efforts remain obscured by history. In the usual picture, historical development refers to the emergence of the forms we now have; the possibility that we might have had others, the serious challenge of alternative models, remains unexplored. But such exploration is of significance; it offers at least the knowledge that some people did not think that the present, as we know it, was inevitable. Their failures provide case studies for contemporary proponents of alternatives.

Nineteenth-century Americans did not have well-established forms of social organization to attack. Consequently, they expressed their alternative visions as they self-consciously built a society. In fact, the creation of institutions preoccupied early-nineteenth-century Americans. Whether they were building banks or railroads, political parties or factories, hospitals or schools, Americans confronted the inappropriateness of traditional European organizational arrangements, and their attempts to find a suitable fit between the form and the context of social life stimulated a prolonged national debate. For the most part, the public record of that controversy rests in massively tedious proposals for the introduction or alteration of particular organizational details; it appears to be the prosaic and even trivial account of practical men solving everyday problems. Yet, the arguments of those practical men over the external features of institutions frequently represented a fundamental clash of social values. The task of appropriately arranging public activities formed an intimate part of the problem of building a nation, and alternative proposals embodied different priorities and dissimilar aspirations for the shape of American society.

Four major alternatives, four models of organization, conflicted in the first half of the nineteenth century. This chapter delineates those models with the data of educational history; the final chapter points to their echoes in the contemporary search for alternatives to public education and in current reform proposals. I call the four models paternalistic voluntarism, democratic localism, corporate voluntarism, and incipient bureaucracy.

In the nineteenth century, as now, the controversy over the shape of education reflected a debate over the shape of society.

Thus the analysis of organizational models, of alternative proposals, provides direct insight into the key value conflicts
within American culture.

The above observation poses a theoretical problem of major
importance: what formulation best describes the varying relationships among social change, social structure, and organizational form? I shall return to the question later and argue,
briefly, that organizations derive their peculiar importance
from their position as mediators between social change and
social structure. I shall try, in the process, to demonstrate a
connection between bureaucracy and social class. Bureaucracy
is not a neutral form; it represents the crystallization of particular social values. In America those values have expressed,
and worked for, class interests.

An initial caution about the four models is in order: They
are not ideal types. Real and fully developed instances of each
can be located. However, that is not to say that in all, or even
most, cases pure and unadulterated forms existed. On the contrary, organizational forms often had features of more than
one model, although in such instances the features of one
were almost always dominant and provided the tone. In the
first part of the analysis that follows I shall discuss pure instances of each model. Later I shall return to the problem of
overlap.

For the most part, the debate centered on objective questions—that is, definite structural characteristics on which organizations may be said to differ. The primary dimensions in
controversy were scale (or size), control, professionalism, and
finance. Each proposal concerning one of these organizational
characteristics rested on social values, which, although often
remaining implicit, had enormous emotional significance. (We
have only to recall the decentralization controversy in New
York today to realize the emotionally laden value content of
issues of control and professionalism in education.) At the
same time, issues of value often explicitly enveloped the de-

bate, especially when the proponents raised questions of organizational purpose. And here the issue most frequently in dispute became the degree of standardization that was desirable in American institutional forms, behavior, and cultural values.

Paternalistic Voluntarism

The New York Public School Society represents the paradigm of paternalistic voluntarism in educational organization. Established as the New York Free School Society in 1805, it stated its purpose as "extending the means of education to such poor children as do not belong to, or are not provided for by, any religious society." The Society offered poor children training in the rudiments of literacy and in morality as it unabashedly tried "to counteract the disadvantages resulting from the situation of their parents." Despite its use of the term "free school," it should be noted, the Society did not advocate tax-supported education in our contemporary sense. Rather, it promoted free schooling only for the very poor.

For almost twenty years, the Society's members aimed but to be "humble gleaners in the wide field of benevolence," touching only the unchurched poor, "such objects . . . as are left by those who have gone before." However, by 1825 the Society had reversed its goal and argued that "it is totally incompatible with our republican institutions, and a dangerous precedent" to allow any portion of the public money to be spent "by the clergy or church trustees for the support of sectarian education." The organization had come to this position partly through participating in an acrimonious controversy involving the alleged misappropriation of educational funds by the Bethel Baptists, who, it was charged, used their share of the state education grant to build a church rather than a school. The interdenominational bickering that resulted convinced the Society that only the establishment of a single nonsectarian educational agency for the entire city could "pre-

vent strife and jealousy and preserve the harmony which has
heretofore so happily existed between the several religious societies in this place."

The generally low quality of small private schools and the
evident dissatisfaction of many parents with existing school
facilities combined to bolster the Society's claim that a major
reorganization of education within New York City had become imperative. Never modest, the Society proclaimed itself
the most appropriate agency to assume the task of educating
all the city's children, offering in support of its claim "an experience of nineteen years, during which period it has educated more than twenty thousand of our poor children." The
legislature accepted the claim of the Society, which became
the New York Public School Society and, as such, began to
disburse virtually the entire public grant for elementary education in the City of New York.

Throughout both phases of its history, voluntarism underlay
the organization of the Society, which was administered by
an unpaid, self-perpetuating board of first citizens who, "having a desire to serve mankind, associate together" and "offer
themselves to the public as agents to carry out certain benevolent purposes," doing so " 'without money and without
price' " as "servants" of the people. It was precisely this fact,
the unrewarded and disinterested dedication of "that class of
men" found in "large cities . . . having leisure and . . . benevolent feelings, who may not wish to mingle in the contest
of politics . . . but who desire to devote themselves to some
good and benevolent objective . . . and in a quiet way accomplish something for the benefit of mankind"—the enlist-
ment of the energy of this class of distinguished citizens, who
would not stoop to practice democratic politics—that gave this
form of organization its distinctive virtues in the eyes of its
champions.

The Society exemplified voluntarism, and therein lay the
source of its success: "All experience *will* demonstrate, that

public objects are better accomplished by these voluntary servants, than they are usually accomplished by persons chosen directly by the people." Voluntarism in practice embodied honesty and zeal. Between 1813 and 1840 the Society spent more than $1 million and "like faithful servants . . . accounted for every cent." In the process of distributing funds, the Society's members had revealed an enthusiastic interest in the cause of education that no paid agent could ever match; during a representative year they "themselves visited the schools *eleven thousand times*." "Point out to me," challenged a Society champion, "your school commissioners who, receiving pay, have done such service." And, he asked a basically hostile audience, "will you, as wise men, say we shall avail ourselves of these voluntary services, or shall we mingle every thing in the turmoil of politics?"

To the supporters of the Public School Society, voluntarism remained a variety of *noblesse oblige*; it rested on faith in the individual talented amateur and, at an over-all administrative level, scorned the need for elaborate organization, state control, or professional staff. As its defenders pointed out, from at least one perspective paternalistic voluntarism worked extremely well. With minimal administrative expense, scrupulous financial integrity, and commendable efficiency, the society maintained for decades an extensive network of schools that taught thousands of children a year.

But make no mistake about it: This was a class system of education. It provided a vehicle for the efforts of one class to civilize another and thereby ensure that society would remain tolerable, orderly, and safe. To the Society, the alarmingly low level of school attendance reflected "either . . . the extreme indigence of the parents . . . or their intemperance or vice; or . . . a blind indifference to the best interests of their offspring." Thus nurtured in "ignorance and amidst the contagion of bad example," these urchins, "instead of being useful members of the community, will become the burdens and pests of society." One method of class civilization employed by the Society was the instruction of parents through public addresses, in which the poor were admonished to "use all endeavors to preserve [their children in] innocency" and to practice temperance, industry, piety, frugality, and, of course, cleanliness, without which "your enjoyments as well as your reputation will be impaired."

But the schools themselves obviously constituted the major agency of class civilization. Within the schools, the particular form of pedagogy applied clearly reflected the Society's goals and its perception of its clients. The Society offered mass education on the cheapest possible plan, the monitorial or Lancasterian system, which counterbalanced a lack of central organization with rigid internal arrangements for each school. In this system, one master instructed a number of older pupils, who, in turn, taught younger ones carefully prescribed lessons. Discipline was strict, based often on shame and the use of humiliating punishments. Competition among students was keenly promoted. The schools were enormous one-room affairs, often with several hundred students and only one master. As De Witt Clinton put the case enthusiastically in 1809, the Lancasterian system "is, in education, what the . . . machines for abridging labor and expense are in the mechanic arts." The system arrived "at its object with the least possible trouble and at the least possible expense." Aside from its minuscule cost per pupil, this mechanistic form of pedagogy, which reduced education to drill, seemed appropriate because the schools served lower-class children who could without offense be likened to unfinished products, needing to be inculcated with norms of docility, cleanliness, sobriety, and obedience.

In Lancasterian schools, "solitary study" did not exist; children were "taught in companies." Teachers and monitors worked to instill "constant habits of attention and vigilance," and an "ardent spirit of emulation [was] kept continually alive. . . . The discipline of the school is enforced by shame, rather than inflicted by pain." It is not difficult to see a very particular ideal of an urban working class implicit in those pedagogical arrangements. As a result of such schooling, the working class would be alert, obedient, and so thoroughly attuned to discipline through group sanctions that a minimum of policing would ensure the preservation of social order. But, and this is important, programmed from an early age to compete with one another, working-class children would not grow up to form a cohesive and threatening class force. The zealous amateurs of the New York Public School Society, it thus becomes apparent, did not design their system for their own children or for the children of their friends. Rather, they attempted to ensure social order through the socialization of the poor in cheap, mass schooling factories.

Critics of paternalistic voluntarism stressed three defects. First, it devolved "upon a private corporation the discharge of an important function of government, without a direct and immediate responsibility to the people." In that respect it was undemocratic and exemplified "a principle . . . hostile to the whole spirit of our institutions." The basis of the democratic theory of public organizations was a belief in the "competency" of the people "to manage all the affairs of government." Thus, to deny them the ability to "determine on the mode, manner, and extent of instruction to be given to their offspring" amounted to overturning "the foundation of our whole system."

More than that, according to its critics, the New York Public School Society was "not a *voluntary system*, in the fullest and broadest meaning of the term." The plan of the Society perverted the notion of voluntarism, because it assumed "exclusive control" of children without permitting their parents any participation whatsoever in "the direction of the course of studies, the management of the schools or . . . the selection of teachers." The Society ordered parents, with "no action or cooperation," to "submit their children to the government and guidance of others, probably strangers, who are in no way accountable to those parents."

The attack on the antivoluntarist nature of the Society signaled a shift in the meaning of voluntarism, which by the 1840's in the American context no longer found favorable expression through *noblesse oblige*. By then, voluntarism had come to mean willingly offered participation in the conduct of institutions owned and managed by elected public representatives. In one sense, the repudiation of paternalistic voluntarism was part of the general attack on monopolies that characterized public discourse in Jacksonian America.

According to its critics, paternalistic voluntarism ignored the variety of American life and reflected an unacceptable cultural bias by imposing uniform services upon a diverse clientele. Although it was often couched in religious terms, the criticism showed a perception of important cultural differences of which religious doctrines served as symptoms. To the opponents of the Society, religious differences represented one form of cultural variation toward which a democratic state had to remain neutral. Therein rested a dilemma: Schools were culturally sensitive institutions; by definition, they touched the areas of irreconcilable difference between denominations. The result was an inverse relation between the size of the school system and the degree of satisfaction it could offer its clientele. It was in that respect, critics argued, that the advantage lay with county school districts, in which small and relatively homogeneous groups controlled and shaped local schools to suit their own preferences. Here, too, lay the defect of the New York Public School Society, which, simply because of the scale of its operation, could never satisfy the various publics of New York City. The defect, critics made clear, inhered not in the peculiarly insensitive behavior of the Society so much as in faults endemic to large organizations. "The defect is one which, so far from being peculiar to the Public School Society, is necessarily inherent in every form of organization which places under one control large masses of discordant materials, which, from the nature of things, cannot submit to any control." An educational agency that could not adapt to the variety of urban life, from this point of view, clearly violated the criteria for free and democratic institutions.

Animosity toward upper-class benevolence underscored both religious and political denunciations of paternalistic voluntarism. A Catholic spokesman, Bishop Hughes, argued that the class bias inherent in the New York Public School Society alienated poor Catholic children and their parents. To the assertion that the schools had the confidence of all classes, Hughes countered that the Society had been so ineffective in overcoming the reluctance of poor parents to send their children to its schools that it had applied for "a legal enactment . . . to compel an attendance." Class resentment, as much as religious resentment, underlay Hughes's bitter observation that the Society had obtained "two enactments from the Common Council, depriving the parents, in time of need—even when cold and starvation have set in upon them—of public relief, unless the children were sent to those or some other schools." So concerned with the problem of attendance had the Society become that it urged "ladies . . . to obtain [the] confidence [of the poor] by soothing words" and "employers to make [school attendance] the condition of employment." "Yet, after all this," Hughes scoffed, "they pretend that they have the confidence of the poor."

Bourgeois hostility toward paternalistic voluntarism bore a relationship to working-class antagonism. Through the existence of organizations such as the Public School Society, free education, public education, and the monitorial system had all become identified with lower-class education. When a New Jersey teacher first observed the monitorial system in the 1820's, he supposed that it was "particularly appropriate to large schools of the poor." However, after studying its operation for a time, he changed his mind and returned to New

Jersey to open a monitorial school for children of all classes. "But I found the rich sent poor children to me, and withheld their own. They had the common ideas about the system." His school lasted but twelve weeks.

An attempt to dissociate public and pauper underlay the free-school movement. Pennsylvania offers a case in point: The constitution of 1790 provided free education only for the poor, and free education had thus come to be associated with charity. In the 1830's the state legislature passed permissive legislation allowing local school districts to introduce free schools for all children. When representatives to the state constitutional convention of 1837–38 tried to enshrine this principle in the revised constitution, a full-scale debate (in which the free-school forces lost) ensued. Both sides to the debate, it is important to remember, professed allegiance to the idea of universal education and the provision of education without cost to those unable to pay. But the opponents of the free-school legislation had two misgivings about the proposed legislation. For one thing, they disliked the style of imposed social change which it represented, a point to which I shall return. For another, and most relevant here, some simply could not see why the necessity of making a public declaration of poverty would deter anyone from taking advantage of a free education. It was to the insensitivity of this point of view that the free-school proponents addressed most of their arguments. One tried to describe for his colleagues how "a feeling of repugnance" accompanied a public declaration of poverty and "prevented many persons from accepting the means of education." If the people "should be educated at the public expense, only on condition that they [be] certified and recorded as Pauper," then they would surely "refuse to avail themselves of the offer."

Thaddeus Stevens, the leading Pennsylvania advocate of free schools, connected the question with middle-class pride and status anxiety, touching what may have been many a raw

nerve in the dislocations of 1837. Many people with children
to be educated, he pointed out, "may have seen better days—
may have been unfortunate in life, and, by reason of their reduced situation and circumstances, may be unable to educate
their families." "Shall we," he asked the delegates, "do nothing to allay the prejudice, which persons in this condition will
almost surely entertain, against allowing their children to be
educated in public schools?" By his very terminology, Stevens
reached the heart of the problem; only radical reorganization
could expunge the legacy of paternalistic voluntarism and divorce the concepts of public and pauper, thereby providing
institutions acceptable to proud and enterprising parents of
limited means.

Democratic Localism

The first alternative proposed to paternalistic voluntarism
was democratic localism. Its sponsors sought to adapt to the
city an organizational form current in rural areas: the district
or community school. The thorough triumph of a centralized
and bureaucratic form of educational organization has diverted
attention from the historical significance of the democratic
localists and the seriousness with which they propounded
their alternative course for American education. Therefore, it
is worth dwelling on a few examples.

One is the plan offered in the early 1840's by New York's
Secretary of State, John C. Spencer, in his attack on the New
York Public School Society. The problems of New York City,
he argued, arose from a "violation" of the principle underlying
education elsewhere in the state, namely, the operation of the
schools by local districts in which the "whole control" of education remained "to the free and unrestricted action of the
people themselves." Thus, the New York City situation could
be remedied simply by making each ward of the city an independent school district, with exactly the same powers as the

districts in country towns, overseen by a Board of Commis-
sioners with strictly limited powers. Nothing in Spencer's
plan, it is important to point out, would prevent a Catholic
majority in a district from hiring Catholic teachers or from
choosing textbooks sympathetic to their religion. Democratic
localism, like all ideologies, served many functions. One was
to rationalize the drive for Catholic power in much the same
fashion that democratic localism today serves as a theoretical
justification for black power.

The democratic localists were active in Massachusetts as
well, most conspicuously in a legislative committee that, in
1840, wrote a report favoring abolition of the state Board of
Education, founded in 1837 and dominated by Horace Mann
as secretary. Although the Board of Education had powers of recommendation only, the committee warned that
it would soon be "converted into a power of regulation"
through its close association with the legislature. Even if the
powers of the board were limited to collecting and diffusing
information, it should be abolished because of its inefficiency
compared with that of the "voluntary associations of teachers,
which preceded" its existence. "In these voluntary associations
a vast number of persons are interested, a spirit of emulation
exists." This spirit, and with it all educational progress, would
be crushed by teacher conventions called by the state.

In fact, a central Board of Education, the Committee argued, characterized European countries where governments
had to compensate for "the ignorance and incapacity of the administrators of local affairs." There, especially in France and
Prussia, the schools were all modeled "upon one plan, as uniform and exact as the discipline of an army." This, of course,
represented the antithesis of the American idea, which assumed the competence of the people to manage their own
affairs. Hence the Board of Education appeared to be "the
commencement of a system of centralization and of monopoly
of power in a few hands, contrary, in every respect, to the true

spirit of our democratical institutions." The bureaucratic regulations of the board, moreover, created an unnecessary nuisance, forcing teachers to fill out forms when they should be teaching children. In short, the Board would fatally damage Massachusetts education by removing its mainspring: the enthusiasm generated by participatory democracy on a local level. "Any attempt to form all our schools, and all our teachers, upon one model, would destroy all competition—all emulation, and even the spirit of improvement itself."

Orestes Brownson formalized the democratic-localist point of view into a theory of governance of American society. According to Brownson, the "individual State, as well as the Union, should be a confederacy of distinct communities," in which each vital interest remained within the smallest possible unit, of which the very smallest would be the district, "which should always be of a size sufficient to maintain a Grammar School." In education the district should remain always "paramount to the State," and each individual school should be "under the control of a community composed merely of the number of families having children in it." Although Brownson pointed out that education, like other governmental affairs, would be "more efficient" in proportion to the degree of "control" by "families specially interested in it," it is clear that efficiency was not his primary objective. Nor was it the paramount concern of other democratic localists, who subordinated both efficiency and organizational rationality to an emphasis on responsiveness, close public control, and local involvement.

Democratic localists fought, actually, on two fronts: against paternalistic voluntarism, as in their opposition to the New York Public School Society, and against bureaucracy or centralization as well, as in their attack on the Massachusetts Board of Education. Emphasis on the virtues of variety, local adaptability, and the symbiotic relation of school and community permeated both conflicts. In their resistance to bureaucracy, however, two other aspects of the democratic-localist attitude emerged most strongly. One was antiprofessionalism. The localists, unlike the sponsors of the New York Public School Society, were not vaguely indifferent to the concept of the professional educator; they were, instead, hostile and suspicious. Brownson played on the theme that normal schools (which had been introduced quite recently) were a Prussian importation to raise the specter of a cadre of Whiggish teachers learning and then imposing state-defined doctrines. "As soon as they can get their Normal Schools into successful operation," he warned, "they will so arrange it, if they can, that no public school shall be permitted to employ a teacher" not trained in one. Then, goodbye to "all liberty of instruction . . . adieu then to republicanism, to social progress."

Like Brownson, the legislative committee recommending abolition of the Board of Education dismissed normal schools as European institutions unsuited to a free society and destructive of the progress that came from the rivalry of academies and high schools vying to produce the best teachers for common schools. To this the committee added scorn for the whole idea of professional instruction for teachers: "Every person, who has himself undergone a process of instruction, must acquire, by that very process, the art of instructing others"; teachers needed special schools no more than mechanics did. Nor was it desirable to raise the job of school teaching to a "distinct and separate profession," inasmuch as schools were open only three or four months a year. "We may as well have a religion established by law," wrote Brownson, "as a system of education, and the government educate and appoint the pastors of our churches, as well as the instructors of our children."

To the democrats the threat of a state educational apparatus was the essential fault in the centralizing viewpoint: the willingness to impose social change and to force attitudes upon the people. An advocate of a local option system for education in Pennsylvania stressed that it was more important even than the existence of free schools to "adapt the system, as nearly as possible, to the *wishes*, as well as the *wants* of the people. No project, however beneficial may be its anticipated operation, should be forced upon the community by other inducements, than those arising from its own merits." Ultimately, this point of view reflected a faith in the wisdom of the people: "Any system perfectly fitted to the wants of society, cannot long remain unpopular," whereas to force innovation upon the community prematurely "can only produce evil, as it may be the means of preventing the general spread and adoption of a system, intrinsically beneficial." A delegate to the state constitutional convention pinpointed the desire to compel the maintenance of free schools by "gentlemen" who believed that "the mass of the people are not intelligent enough to act upon the subject themselves."

The case of the democratic localists, then, rested ultimately on a combination of faith in the people and a point of view about the sources of social change. "If we ever expect to root deeply this system in the affection of the people," warned a delegate to the Pennsylvania convention, "we must make the system voluntary—entirely so. But if we force it upon the people, it will be taken with an ill grace, and will be made use of, if used at all, with reluctance and suspicion." To the democratic localist, legislatures should enact, not lead, the public will. If a large minority happened to oppose a solution, however desirable the outcome might seem, it would be folly to legislate until the people had changed their minds. In Pennsylvania, in the last analysis, the most important legislative consideration remained the fact that "the prejudices against this system of education are very strong." The imposition of social change would never work; changes in society, in habits and in attitudes, came only from within the people themselves as they slowly, haltingly, but surely exercised their innate common sense and intelligence. By being left to their own devices, by perhaps being encouraged, cajoled, and softly educated, but not by being forced, the people would become roused to the importance of universal education and the regular school attendance of their children.

As a proposal for the organization of urban education (for instance, one scheme put forward for New York City), democratic localism flourished for only a short time. Its failure was predictable from the start, for it rested on a distinctly rural point of view. Its proponents did not adapt their viewpoint to the city and hence ignored critical differences between rural and urban contexts and the special problems the latter posed for the conduct of education, points to which I shall return. Nor did its sponsors—for instance, Berkshire Congregationalists in Massachusetts—see the ironically undemocratic possibilities inherent in giving free rein to local majorities.

Democratic localism referred at once to an intellectual construct and a real situation. Its problem was the lack of congruence between the two. As an intellectual construct, it offered a simple explanation and a simple cure for feelings of powerlessness and dislocation induced by the rapid social change of the 1830's and 1840's. But, unfortunately, it rested on a nostalgic memory whose relationship to reality was, at best, problematical. For was the small rural town the warm, enlightened, coherent exemplar of democracy that romantic intellectuals would have us believe? Certainly, at its worst, democratic localism in action was the tyrannical local majority whose ambition was control and the dominance of its own narrow sectarian or political bias in the schoolroom. Orestes Brownson notwithstanding, the people of the Berkshires probably concerned themselves more with the problem of putting orthodox texts into the classroom than with the theory of federalism. Whatever John C. Spencer believed, democratic localism at one level rationalized the Catholic desire to run Catholic schools with public money. More often than its theoretical exponents would care to admit, the reality of democratic localism came closer to the Hoosier School Master than to Brownson's portrait. Walking into Flat Crick, Indiana, in search of a teaching job, Ralph Hartsook confronted one of the local trustees, "old Jack Means":

> "Want to be a school-master, do you? Well, what would *you* do in Flat Crick deestrick, *I'd* like to know? Why, the boys have driv off the last two, and licked the one afore them like blazes. . . . They'd pitch you out of doors, sonny, neck and heels, afore Christmas. . . .
>
> "You see," continued Mr. Means, spitting in a meditative sort of way, "you see, we a'n't none of your saft sort in these diggins. It takes a *man* to boss this deestrick. Howsudever, ef you think you kin trust your hide in Flat Crick school-house, I ha'n't got no 'bjection. . . . Any other trustees? Wal, yes. But as I pay the most taxes, t'others jist let me run the thing."

Nevertheless, despite its intellectual softness, democratic localism at its best provided a noble alternative vision: It embraced a broad and humanistic conception of education as uncharacteristic of nineteenth-century as of twentieth-century schools and schoolmen. Consider, for example, Brownson's exhortation, which eschewed the specially utilitarian in education in terms of a distinctively American social structure:

> Here professions and pursuits are merely the accidents of individual life. Behind them we recognize Humanity, as paramount to them all. Here man, in theory at least, is professor. Professions and pursuits may be changed according to judgment, will, or caprice, as circumstances permit, or render necessary or advisable. Consequently, here we want an education for that which is permanent in man, which contemplates him as back of all the accidents of life, and which shall be equally valuable to him whatever be the mutations which go on around him, the means he may choose or be compelled to adopt to obtain a livelihood.

The education of importance thus was "general education" or the "education of Humanity," education that "fits us for our destiny, to attain our end as simple human beings."

Corporate Voluntarism

A third model, coexistent with paternalistic voluntarism and democratic localism, was corporate voluntarism, the conduct of *single* institutions as individual corporations operated by self-perpetuating boards of trustees and financed either wholly through endowment or through a combination of endowment and tuition. Corporate voluntarism characterized primarily secondary and higher education, academies and colleges. As is the case with democratic localism, the victory of the public secondary school as we know it today obscures the seriousness with which many nineteenth-century educational promoters considered corporate voluntarism as an alternative model. In fact, for a time it appeared as though corporate voluntarism in the shape of academies would become the general pattern for secondary education.

Between the late eighteenth and early nineteenth centuries, the academy became the dominant institution for secondary education throughout the country. In certain ways the academy represented little that was novel. Private schools had existed throughout most of the colonial period. Some taught classical studies; others provided the only formal source of more directly vocational education, particularly in surveying, navigation, and bookkeeping, as well as English grammar and mathematics. The curricular novelty of academies rested on their combination of the two sorts of studies, classical and modern, in the same school. Administratively, the novelty of the academy lay in the wide diffusion of a particular form of organization, which had existed earlier in only a limited number of instances; this was the corporate form. The more permanent and larger academies throughout the country generally began with boards of trustees who raised money, hired a schoolmaster, obtained incorporation by the state, and continued as general managers and overseers of the school.

States accepted the corporate form of organization for secondary education as desirable public policy and actively promoted its diffusion through grants of land or money to individual academies. States conceived of academies as public institutions; in the early republican period, "public" implied the performance of broad social functions and the service of a large, heterogeneous, nonexclusive clientele rather than control and ownership by the community or state. In this respect, the policy of Massachusetts is particularly instructive, because it represents so radical a departure from the active promotion of grammar-school maintenance by towns, which had been the practice in the seventeenth and earlier eighteenth centuries.

A committee of the legislature recommended in 1797 that the state use land grants to promote the establishment of academies in each county; proponents of the measure argued that by assisting and encouraging incorporated academies the state could fulfill its obligation to ensure the existence of facilities for secondary education. Consequently, Massachusetts began a system of land grants to academies that lasted well into the nineteenth century. As late as 1838, similar arguments launched the state of Pennsylvania on an active campaign of academy assistance. These examples reveal the inadequacy of any sharp dichotomy between public and private in the early nineteenth century. Although managed and owned by self-perpetuating boards of trustees, academies were profoundly public institutions.

The policy of public encouragement and the corporate form marked academy development throughout the country. However, to ascribe very much unity to the academy movement or to academy features is misleading. As the name "academy" became fashionable, standards for its application progressively loosened until it covered most of the small, very private, and often transient schools, which far outnumbered incorporated academies. Similarly, other generalizations break down: Academies were not entirely urban or rural, boarding or day, denominational or secular. Denominations actively established academies as well as colleges, and ministers took a prominent role in their promotion and also as academy masters. The academy curriculum likewise virtually defies generalizations. Some academies stressed college preparation and hence classical studies; most included English studies as well; and many offered a secondary education to youth bound for an immediate career in commerce rather than college. The actual curricula themselves consisted of dazzling varieties of specific subjects.

The diversity that colors every aspect of an academy portrait leaves a great many questions. Hard data on a number of critical issues, such as the social background of students and the role of academies in social mobility, are lacking. Any explanation of the remarkable proliferation of academies and of their significance must be tentative at this juncture. From the point of view of state legislatures, academies must have appeared to be delightfully inexpensive and administratively simple; without the need to raise taxes, a relatively small public investment ensured the maintenance of substantial numbers of secondary schools. The tasks of founding, managing, and supervising the schools, moreover, rested with self-contained boards of trustees and thus added insignificantly to the burdens of the state. The corporate mode of control was congruent with contemporary arrangements for managing other forms of public business. As states turned from mercantilist regulation of the economy, they adopted a liberal stance that identified the public interest with unrestricted privileges of incorporation and removal of regulations governing economic activity. The argument that autonomous, competing corporations, aided but not controlled by the state, best served the public interest extended easily from finance, travel, and manufacturing to education. Academies were educational corporations.

Controversies between the supporters of academies and the advocates of public high schools provide the most explicit example of the debate over corporate voluntarism. One of the most interesting took place in 1856 and 1857 between the sponsors of the Norwich (Connecticut) Free Academy, especially the Reverend J. P. Gulliver, and the editor of the *Massachusetts Teacher*, a vigorous champion of public high schools, then more numerous in Massachusetts than in any other state. According to Gulliver, the movement for educational reform, which began in New England in the 1830's, continually encountered frustration. Especial hostility met the proposal to establish a public high school, which was defeated by the votes of the poor:

> A few (but only a few) of the heavy tax-payers were the first to smell treason. They passed the word to a set of men, who flourish in their own esteem, by exhibiting their powers in thwarting what others attempt to do. The usual cry was raised, "a school for the rich!" The prejudices of poor men were appealed to. This very class, who were to be most benefited by the change, were excited to oppose it.

Thus did the measure fail and the cause of educational improvement languish in Norwich until a group of wealthy men determined to take the initiative by uniting to "establish a high school and endow it, which should be open, free of all charge, to all classes." This they did, and the Norwich Free Academy, well financed, carefully planned, educationally progressive, opened in 1856. It was the clearest example in the country, its sponsors well knew, of an alternative to the public high school.

The sponsors of the school did not hesitate to point out the implications of its successful establishment. "There is no subject," asserted Gulliver, "which more imperatively demands examination at the present moment than the expediency of endowments for literary and educational purposes. The attention of men of wealth all over the country is now directed with great interest to the subject." Gulliver had no doubt that the Free Academy had provided a practical demonstration of the virtues offered by endowment and essentially private management, thus setting the issue. As he made his case, Gulliver echoed in part the champions of the New York Public School Society when they cited its virtues:

Honesty. Never had there been reported a case of misappropriation of funds on the part of a self-perpetuating board of trustees. *Enlightened management.* The public simply lacked the competence to conduct secondary schools. Public discourse, said Gulliver, too often degenerated into "talk about 'popular sovereignty' and the rights of the people to manage everything that in any way affects their interests—which is nothing but miserable cant." After all, why not allow the people to manage banks or insurance companies, Gulliver asked. Or why not give to the town meeting the management of "manufacturing corporations, benevolent societies, philanthropic institutions, military organizations, and ships' crews"? Clearly, to do so would be absurd; thus it implied no denigration of the people to assert their incapacity to manage "a school for instruction in the ancient and modern languages, the higher mathematics, the sciences, and the fine arts." In short, endowment lifted education out of politics and assured it competent direction.

Edward Hitchcock, President of Amherst College, stressed a related theme within the concept of corporate voluntarism: the congruence between the flexibility of essentially private institutions and the variability of American conditions. Like the democratic localists, proponents of corporate voluntarism assumed that "systems of education ought to be wisely suited to the character and condition of the people among whom they are introduced." From that assumption the corporate-voluntarist argument proceeded along two lines: "Freedom from governmental interference with our literary institutions" as a basic principle underscored the right of the parent to select his child's education, which, in turn, found expression in the establishment of academies of varying types, suited to varying tastes. To exchange this mild anarchy for a state system of secondary schools would produce a "treadmill system" that was nothing but a "wretched substitute." The other line emanating from the original premise related the individuality of the American character to the varied degrees of civilization across the country. Both arguments called for an educational system that could sensitively reflect and adequately provide for personal and cultural idiosyncrasies. One of the "excellencies" of the academies, Hitchcock submitted, was that "they can conform to all the irregular demands of society, without destroying their individuality."

Although Hitchcock may have been rationalizing low academic quality, corporate voluntarism did seem to combine the virtues of the other two models. Without the stigma of lower-class affiliation, it offered disinterested, enlightened, and continuous management that kept the operation of education out of the rough and unpredictable field of politics. At the same time, by placing each institution under a different administrative authority, it retained the limited scope essential to institutional variety, flexibility, and adaptation to local circumstance.

Academies represented the quintessence of voluntarism as *noblesse oblige*, because they rapidly diffused throughout the country a combination of public goals and private control wrapped in the mantle of disinterested service. But the emergence of a new definition of "public school" signaled the demise of corporate voluntarism as public policy. George Boutwell, one-time Governor of Massachusetts, secretary of the Board of Education, and eventually United States Senator, stated the matter with precision: "A *public school* I understand to be a school established by the public—supported chiefly or entirely by the public, controlled by the public, and accessible to the public upon terms of equality, without special charge for tuition." With great care he went on to specify why the Norwich Free Academy and similar schools could not be considered public. Although they were "sometimes, upon a superficial view, supposed to be public," schools of that sort were only "public in their use, but not in their foundation or control, and are therefore not public schools." Academies could not be considered public schools, and in the context of the times "public" had become a necessary label. Thus, as it became apparent that only institutions financed by the community or state and directly controlled by its officers merited that definition, both paternalistic and corporate voluntarism were doomed.

Incipient Bureaucracy

Among the competing organizational models, incipient bureaucracy triumphed. The promoters of bureaucracy, including the great figures of the "educational revival," like Horace Mann and Henry Barnard, concentrated on attacking democratic localism, which was the chief hindrance to their schemes. They struck first at the notion that democratic localism was in fact democratic by pointing out that it would permit 51 per cent of the local parents to dictate the religious, moral, and political ideas taught to the children of the remainder. The proponents of democratic localism erred in assuming the widespread existence of homogeneous potential units of school administration. In actuality, the variety within most communities, city wards, or neighborhoods would foster intensely political competition for control of the local school in order to ensure the propagation of particular points of view, or, at the least, the exclusion of rival ones. "If one man claimed to have his peculiar doctrines taught, why not another?" asked Horace

Mann. "Why not all?—until you would have a Babel of creeds in the same school, which a heathen would be ashamed of." Similarly, the Free School Society warned: "If religious societies are to be the only participators of the portion of the school fund for the city of New York, a spirit of rivalry will . . . be excited between different sects, which will go to disturb the harmony of society, and which will early infuse strong prejudices in the minds of children taught in the different schools." Aside from the debilitating effect of political struggle upon education, the result could easily abridge the liberties of parents by forcing them to choose between submitting their children to alien points of view and arranging for expensive private schooling.

The second defect of democratic localism was, as I have noted, a rural bias, which overlooked the special educational problems posed by cities. Population growth and heterogeneity made extremely decentralized administration inefficient in an urban setting, because the existence of "two or more independent . . . half belligerent and jealous districts" and "a double or treble set of officers" represented an uneconomical duplication of facilities and units, which would squander financial resources. Democratic localism within a city encouraged an inequitable situation as well, for it allowed a lack of parity in educational facilities and standards within a relatively small geographical area. Thus, the improvement of the "territorial and administrative agencies, and organization of our common schools so as to enable all the people of a city or borough to act on this great interest as they act on their other great interests"—an "immediate union of all the districts"— represented the "first great step" in urban school reform.

The inefficiency of democratic localism prevented the schools from undertaking the distinctive tasks assigned them in urban settings. School reformers perceived the city through an ambivalent and nostalgic lens, which registered modern life as

at best a problematical substitute for the pastoral setting of
early New England. Once, there had been "no cities and but
few large towns"; most men lived by "agriculture and the
ruder forms of mechanical labor." By contrast, the "atten-
dants" of modern civilization were "populous cities, narrow
streets, dark lanes, cellar habitations, crowded workshops,
over-filled and over-heated factories, and . . . sedentary pur-
suits that tax and wear and destroy the physical powers, and
undermine the moral and mental." With its "melancholy
train of evils," civilization "is not an unmixed good; and we
cannot offer to the city or the factory any adequate compensation" for the pure and healthful life "which may be enjoyed in
the country villages and agricultural districts."

Whether the compensation could or could not be adequate,
it was to come primarily from one source. For a complex variety of reasons (which I shall consider in Chapter 3), schools
came to be perceived as the key agencies for uplifting the
quality of city life by stemming diffusion of the poverty, crime,
and immorality that were thought to accompany urban and
industrial development. As Henry Barnard phrased the problem: "The condition and improvement of her manufacturing
population, in connection with the education of the whole
people, is at this time the great problem for New England to
work out." Schools had to halt the impending degeneracy of
the New England character and heal the developing class gulf
within New England cities, where existed "poverty, ignorance,
profligacy, and irreligion, and a classification of society as
broad and deep as ever divided the plebian and patrician of
Ancient Rome."

In that setting, the first problem of the schools became, very
simply, to ensure the regular attendance of all children upon a
prolonged, systematic, and carefully structured formal education. Within the city, "so unfavorable" were the "surrounding
circumstances," so "numerous . . . the temptations in the

street, from the example and teaching of low-bred idleness"
that school attendance should begin at the age of five. In fact,
the incompetence of the urban poor as parents implied the
need to exchange the natural for an artificial family setting:

> No one at all familiar with the deficient household arrange-
> ments and deranged machinery of domestic life, of the extreme
> poor, and ignorant, to say nothing of the intemperate—of the
> examples of rude manners, impure and profane language, and
> all the vicious habits of low bred idleness, which abound in
> certain sections of all populous districts—can doubt, that it is
> better for children to be removed as early and as long as pos-
> sible from such scenes and examples.

As might be expected from their image of the urban poor,
school reformers held that "the primary object" in removing
the child from the influence of the parent to the influence of
the school was "not so much . . . intellectual culture, as the
regulation of the feelings and dispositions, the extirpation of
vicious propensities, the preoccupation of the wilderness of
the young heart with the seeds and germs of moral beauty,
and the formation of a lovely and virtuous character by the
habitual practice of cleanliness, delicacy, refinement, good temper, gentleness, kindness, justice, and truth." Under the influence of a surrogate mother, a female teacher, the process
should continue until the age of twelve, at which time working-class children might safely leave school to receive the rest
of their character training in the practical business of earning
a living. The matter of school attendance, warned Barnard,
was not to be taken lightly. Should its neglect continue, society would reap its "retribution" for the "crime of neglected
childhood."

Barnard, it is of great significance to remember, accurately
reflected the sentiment of most people promoting schools.
Nearly without exception, they chose the heart over the head.
Moral education, or the formation of right attitudes, was

more important than learning any skill or subject. Schools existed to serve society by tending the characters of otherwise neglected children.

That task assumed special importance in relation to industrial society. The values to be instilled by the schools were precisely those required for the conduct of a complex urban society—for example, the importance of time. Expressed as the problem of irregular and tardy attendance, the problem of instilling a sense of time into children and their parents obsessed school committees. Aside from the real problems caused by a lack of that sense, the great stress on time indicates a concern that extended beyond the schoolroom. One writer, to make that concern explicit, pointed to the parallel behavior required of the schoolboy and the working man. For both, "precision" had become a necessary habit; "regularity and economy of time" had come to mark "our community, as appears in the running 'on time' of long trains on our great network of railways; the strict regulation of all large manufacturing establishments; as well as the daily arrangements of our school duties." The connection was unmistakable; schools were training grounds for commerce. What had been "instilled in the mind of the pupil" became "thoroughly recognized by the man as of the first importance in the transaction of business."

The problem of time haunts developing societies; it is at the very heart of the transformation of agrarian habits, which do not emphasize precision and promptness, into habits consonant with city life and large-scale manufacture. Every society since the industrial revolution began has had to develop a mechanism for changing the behaviors appropriate in a traditional society into those called for by modernity. America handled that problem, the problem of industrial discipline, like so many others, through the schools. Industrialists, in fact, have not been hesitant about stating what they have wanted. That was clear, to take two instances, in the responses that Horace Mann and George Boutwell received in 1841 and

1859 when they asked manufacturers about the value of educated labor. One wrote that knowledge was secondary to morality, and that educated workers showed "more orderly and respectful . . . deportment," plus a greater willingness "to comply with the . . . regulations of an establishment." During labor disputes, the same experienced capitalist wrote, "I have always looked to the most intelligent, best educated and the most moral for support." It goes without saying that it was "the ignorant and uneducated . . . the most turbulent and troublesome" who acted "under the impulse of excited passion and jealousy." The association of virtues was significant: Education, morality, and docility were all equated; they formed a trinity marking a properly schooled man. If there be any doubt on that point, consider the words of another manufacturer, who praised the "diligence and . . . willing acquiescence" of the educated who, working their way into the confidence of their colleagues, exerted "a conservative influence" in times of labor trouble, an influence "of great value pecuniarily and morally." The common school made company men.

Henry Barnard's complaint of the "want of system" in contemporary education followed from his perception of the moral importance of regular attendance. "What other business of society," he asked, "could escape utter wreck, if conducted with such want of system—with such constant disregard of the fundamental principle of the division of labor?"

Thus, the first generation of urban schoolmen began by rejecting democratic localism and argued for carefully structured systems of education. Fully developed plans for systems of schools and elaborate architecture, curricula, and pedagogy mark the reports and appeals of Mann, Barnard, and their contemporaries. Their goal was to uplift the quality of public education by standardizing and systematizing its structure and content.

All their plans had certain characteristics in common, most

important among them centralization. This had two principal components: first, the modification and eventual elimination of the bastion of democratic localism, the district system, whereby each section of a town or city managed its own schools with a great deal of autonomy. The case against this I have considered above. The ultimate remedy was the replacement of the district by one central board of education. In most cases, however, that was politically impossible, and reformers consequently turned to an interim measure, the establishment of high schools. In Massachusetts, for example, both the law and practical considerations required the high school to be a town school, administered by the town school committee, and siphoning off students from all the districts into the one central institution. It was thus an administrative device for undercutting the power of the districts.

The first high school was Boston English, opened in 1820; by the start of the Civil War, Massachusetts had 103 high schools, or roughly one to every three towns and cities. Other states developed high schools in a sequence that reflected their social development, for high school establishment generally accompanied the diffusion of urban features and attitudes. The first high school in Pennsylvania opened in Philadelphia in 1836; in Wisconsin, in Southport, 1849; in California, in San Francisco, 1856. Wisconsin had eleven high schools in 1865; by that date probably not more than six or seven existed in California.

In most states the initial establishment of high schools preceded both enabling and compulsory legislation. The first Massachusetts law requiring towns of a certain size to maintain a high school was passed in 1827; Pennsylvania did not pass indirectly enabling legislation until 1849; the first enabling laws in Wisconsin were passed in 1856. In each of those states, legislation represented a belated recognition of what had in fact happened, as well as, in some cases, an attempt to diffuse more widely developments already under way.

From their inception, high schools were generally public institutions in our contemporary sense of the word; they were also free and offered both classical and nonclassical courses of study. Except in large cities, high schools were usually coeducational. At first, little standardization of curriculum or internal organization existed among high schools. Some offered two-, some three-, and a few four-year courses. In cities high schools were generally large enough to permit the division of students by grade and, by the 1870's, the employment of specialist teachers in a number of subjects. Likewise, little uniformity existed in the books used, material covered, or standards attained.

The grading of schools formed the second and related component of centralization. In the district system, children of all ages were taught in one room by one teacher. That is precisely what school reformers wanted to end. As Barnard put it, one of the principal "conditions of success" for a system of public schools was a "classification of scholars" that brought "a large number of similar age and attainments, at all times, and in every state of their advancement" together within classrooms under the exclusive charge of the same teacher. Reformers argued that graded schools yielded enormous increases in educational efficiency and effectiveness, and their blueprints featured carefully designed sequences of schools of which a high school formed the apex.

An emphasis on supervision accompanied centralization. The opponents of democratic localism argued eloquently for state boards of education with paid secretaries and, at the local level, for superintendents of schools. In Boston the Annual Visiting Committee in 1845 described a state of administrative anarchy—"twenty-four men, not paid for any labor, who share a responsibility, which, thus broken into fragments, presses no one"—and concluded that the system wholly lacked "permanence, personal responsibility, continued and systematic labor." These elements could be introduced quite readily through the employment of a superintendent, an adequately paid, tenured, full-time administrator. Like the grading of schools, a superintendent would improve educational efficiency and, in addition, would increase the honesty of school operation to a degree that would more than compensate for his salary.

The stress on paid, full-time supervision spilled over into arguments for professional expertise. The emphasis on teacher training and the development of normal schools became an intimate aspect of the bureaucratic strategy. The case for normal schools shared an important assumption with the argument for professional supervision: that education had become a difficult and complex undertaking whose conduct and administration required individuals with specialized talents, knowledge, and experience. As one writer stated the matter: "The man who imagines himself a teacher, qualified for the responsible duties of an instructor, merely because he has seen others teach in a particular way, is just as much an empiric, as a pretender in medicine, who occasionally walks through the wards of a hospital." The "day for quack pedagogues is passed."

Professionalism and system, like the obsession with punctuality, reflected industrial values. Newly industrialized people must learn to reward a man for what he can do rather than for who he is. They must supplant ascription with achievement. The very structure proposed for school systems expressed that goal. Graded schools, regulated promotions, and trained staff were designed to counter problems created by a populace accustomed to gaining privileges by means that had little to do with capacity to perform. Parents, for instance, applied steady pressure to gain admittance to high school for their unqualified children; others circumvented competition by using their wealth to buy advantage for their children in the form of a private education; school committeemen not infrequently gave scarce jobs to indifferently qualified relatives or friends. In short, people mobilized personal influence and pressure, the weight of their position or their money, to gain rewards that their ability could not purchase.

That simply would not do. Unlike traditional societies, with well-defined roles and rigid social structures, societies that are modernizing require a commitment to competence. It is necessary to call forth and reward achievement if specialized and technical tasks are to be performed. The transition from a pre-industrial society requires a shift in the basis of social valuation from ascription to achievement. That became one function of public education, as schoolmen again attempted to facilitate economic change through the transformation of social attitudes.

The content as well as the structure of education presented a problem: how to honor minority sensibilities while inculcating the norms required for upright and orderly social living. The official response to the problem of minority sensibility was to proclaim the school religiously and politically neutral. "The great ideal" of the common school system, Horace Mann pointed out, is "that those points of doctrine, or faith, upon which good and great men differ, shall not be obtruded into this mutual ground of the schools." In practice the schools did not become neutral, as Catholic spokesmen all knew. Protestant ministers, as David Tyack has shown, played active and important roles in common-school promotion and management, and it is in fact impossible to disentangle Protestantism from the early history of the common school, which exuded an unmistakable chauvinistic pan-Protestant tone.

The class bias of education, however, was even more pervasive than its tepid Protestant tone. A configuration of moral and cultural values best described as mid-Victorian permeated school textbooks and statements of educational objectives, such as the following one, entitled "The Necessity of Restraint." Children, lamented the author (whose basic goal, like that of other reformers, might without too much distortion be termed the extirpation of sexuality) "have not learned that present self-denial is the price at which future good is often to be obtained, and that present suffering and toil are rewarded by subsequent enjoyment. These lessons the child *must* learn." Without restraint and direction, the child would become "the victim of passion, and having no rule over his own spirits, he would be exposed to fearful moral dangers." Untamed human nature, to this frightened author, strove continually to break loose into an unbridled orgy of passionate sensual indulgence. Without restraint, "without these counter-checks upon the passions," the author asked, "what would our race be?"

Thus, sublimation became the goal of public education. In 1858, for instance, the Boston Public School Committee admonished parents that "every pure and refined pleasure for which a child acquires a relish, is to that extent, a safeguard against a low and debasing one." It became a key function of the schools to teach the substitution of higher for lower pleasures, which, from one point of view, represented a systematic attempt to diffuse sexual repression throughout society. "Passionate" and "sensual" became two of the most pejorative words in educational discourse. "Those, whose minds and whose hearts have been properly trained and disciplined by education, have control over their passions. Having cultivated a taste for simple and innocent pleasures, rather than a love for vicious excitement, their desires are awakened by objects higher than any gratification merely animal." In their objectives for education, schoolmen thus reflected a peculiarly Victorian combination of sexual and status anxiety that forms one of the least lovely aspects of nineteenth-century culture. Whether that came from their own discomfort at suspecting mass indulgence of pleasures that they themselves had painfully renounced or from a desire for social control, it was apparent that the traits of character schoolmen found necessary to fit the working class for upright urban living represented an idealized Victorian middle-class portrait of itself. It is apparent, too, that public schools represented an attempt to effect a massive and permanent desexualization of society.

Herein lies an irony: Schoolmen who thought they were promoting a neutral and classless—indeed, a *common*—school education remained unwilling to perceive the extent of cultural bias inherent in their own writing and activity. However, the bias was central and not incidental to the standardization and administrative rationalization of public education. For, in the last analysis, the rejection of democratic localism rested only partly on its inefficiency and violation of parental prerogative. It stemmed equally from a gut fear of the cultural divisiveness inherent in the increasing religious and ethnic diversity of American life. Cultural homogenization played counterpoint to administrative rationality. Bureaucracy was intended to standardize far more than the conduct of public life.

An instructive instance of the above point is a debate in Pennsylvania regarding the degree of official sanction to be given to the German language. Said one speaker, "I think . . . that we ought no longer to be divided into separate races, and by distinct languages and habits." Another put the matter even more bluntly: "I think that the whole people of the state should be amalgamated as soon as that end can possibly be accomplished." It was, after all, implicit in the "common" of "common school" that education should forge social unity by blurring cultural distinctiveness—the familiar idea of the melting pot.

What is less obvious, although closely related, is the racist implication of such a point of view. If an attitude that considers one group to be different from and inferior to another in some basic and essential fashion can be labeled racist, then we are forced to the conclusion that racist sentiment scarred the origins of public education. For it is in precisely those terms—difference and inferiority—that school people perceived lower-class children. Take, for example, this description of its task offered by the Boston School Committee:

> taking children at random from a great city, undisciplined, uninstructed, often with inveterate forwardness and obstinacy, and with the inherited stupidity of centuries of ignorant ancestors; forming them from animals into intellectual beings; and, so far as a school can do it, from intellectual beings into spiritual beings; giving to many their first appreciation of what is wise, what is true, what is lovely, and what is pure; and not merely their first impressions, but what may possibly be their only impressions.

Now, the Boston School Committee was not exceptional in its perception of immigrant children. Nor was the task it described incidental to its work. As the earlier arguments from Boutwell and Barnard make clear, the urban public school had been founded to cope with the problems of urban living, among which the threat of the urban poor had high priority. It approached this task from a racist perspective on its clientele. Thus racism, like antisexuality, is integral, not incidental, to the very structure of public education. In the course of a century, the particular object has changed from Irish Catholic to black, but the attitude remains.

It was partly to deal effectively with the problem of the urban poor that bureaucracy developed as the mode of organizing urban schools. The racism thus integral to bureaucratic structure became even more deeply entrenched, because it early acquired a functional utility as a defense of bureaucratic failure. In 1876 one commentator related an alleged decrease in the standard of educational attainment to the altered background of students. No longer did they come from rural New England families, where cultivated common sense and native intelligence were the rule. Instead, the "material" that the schools were "required to shape and polish" derived from different and inferior sources:

> A very large proportion of the pupils in our cities and populous towns come from homes utterly destitute of culture, and of the means and the spirit of culture, where a book is never seen, and reading is with the adult members a lost art, or one never acquired. There are schools in which four-fifths or more of the children are of this class. I at one time had under my supervision a school in which ninety-nine percent of the children were of foreign parentage, and hardly one of the whole from a home level with the lowest status of native-born intelligence. In such minds a sunken foundation must be laid by months or years of unpromising toil, before any portion of the work begins to appear above the surface. It seems almost impossible to give them a conception of either the uses or the pleasures of knowledge, or to lead them to that primal exercise of judgment by which two ideas are compared or combined. Even the simplest object-lessons are often unintelligible to them. Instruction can hardly be conveyed to them in terms which they can understand, and in what they attempt to learn, memory derives no assistance from association. A person of exceptional skill and patience might hope out of a single such block in the lapse of years to carve a statue; but what shall we think of the sculptor who is compelled every day to make some strokes of the chisel on forty or fifty of them?

What, indeed, but to excuse his failure? That this essentially racist excuse for educational failure is reminiscent of contemporary discourse about cultural deprivation is not an accident, for the contemporary notion is but a continuation of the old: a well-developed bureaucratic strategy for explaining educational disaster by reference to the inferiority of the pupils.

Irony and class bias emerge from the early history of the high school as well as from general statements of educational purpose. For the goals and claims of high school promoters bore only a tangential relation to the facts of high school attendance and function. High school promoters coupled arguments for centralization and general educational uplift with the assertion that public secondary schools would foster the economic prosperity of the community by attracting settlers, increasing land values, and providing properly trained recruits for higher branches of industrial and commercial employment. At the same time, the influence of the high school would radiate to the community as a whole, diffusing culture among the people. Like the common schools, moreover, high schools were expected by their advocates to gather together children of all social classes and thereby promote social harmony and justice. In the high school, poor and also middle-class parents might have an opportunity to secure the advancement of their children without paying tuition; it provided an education that would foster social mobility and insure individual prosperity in a time of bewildering economic flux. For girls, the high school offered excellent preparation for schoolteaching, the most desirable occupation to which they could realistically aspire.

What little evidence exists of an actual connection between high school attendance and middle-class employment in the mid-nineteenth century seems to indicate that the schools did offer some advantages to boys in search of white-collar work. Unquestionably, they served girls in search of teaching jobs, and female students generally far outnumbered male. However, contrary to popular belief, in its early history the high school was not popular with the working class, which frequently viewed it as a class institution irrelevant to its own aspirations and impossible to utilize when the earnings of adolescents were needed to keep the family alive. Nor, in its early history, did the high school actively promote social mobility, social harmony, or egalitarianism. Very few poor children attended; indeed, only a very small minority of the community's children even began high school, and most of them left before graduation. It was wealthy, prestigious community leaders concerned with economic development and social integration, as well as middle-class parents concerned with mobility and educational expense, who formed the nucleus of high school promoters. In the long run, the high school replaced the academy as the dominant institution for secondary education because it offered middle-class parents a means of educating their children at public expense and keeping them home during the process. At the same time, it perpetuated the differential advantages of middle-class children and may actually have served as a social sorting device, limiting rather than promoting mobility. Certainly, in some instances, the attempt to institute a high school split a community along class lines and, ironically, fostered estrangement between school and community and between social groups, a consequence precisely opposite to the one desired and anticipated by high school supporters.

The movement of the bureaucrats in the ante bellum period was not entirely toward order and rigid system; their proposals for the actual conduct of classes and the reform of pedagogy moved in the other direction. In this they represented the opposite of the paternalistic voluntarists, who, as we have observed, combined a relative lack of external order with a rigid internal system of teaching. To the common-school revivalists, the term "mechanical," as applied to pedagogy, was thoroughly pejorative. As they systematized the administration and grading of schools, these reformers, for a complex variety of reasons, argued for a softening of pedagogy rooted in the substitution of the arousal of interest, affection for the teacher, and internalization of the desire to learn for interpersonal competition (or "emulation") and corporal punishment as sources of motivation. As one writer stated the case, motivating children necessitated *"exciting their curiosity."* The model teacher connected "with his instruction, as far as possible, what is interesting and attractive so that the associations, formed in the minds of his pupils, will leave them in love with the subject of investigation, and in the proper time, bring them back to the pursuit with readiness and alacrity." The pupil, of course, "must be made to work; but he must work voluntarily, cheerfully, with hope." In that way, the model for the teacher-pupil relation became the relation of parent and child at its finest, both firm and affectionate.

In one other crucial way the leading figures of the educational revival did not behave like traditional bureaucrats: They did not adopt the bureaucratic ideal of personality. Neither their ideal teacher nor their ideal administrator was a gray, colorless public servant efficiently and quietly executing the public will. Quite the contrary: The model for the educational administrator came neither from business nor the military but from evangelical religion. It was not a coincidence that the period of mid-century reform was called, even at the time, the educational revival. It was to be a secular evangelism. To Horace Mann, educational reform was not a task or a necessity but—and this word constantly permeates his published and unpublished writing—a "cause." Nowhere is the evangelical impulse at the heart of the educational revival more evident than in Mann's letters of encouragement to Henry Barnard. "I rejoice," he wrote, "to learn that Connecticut is engaged in the work of education. . . . What cause can be nobler? What cause holds in its embrace so much of the well-being of the future millions? . . . I welcome you as a fellow laborer in the cause of education." Writing of his strain during the attempt to abolish the Board of Education in 1840, Mann told Barnard that he found his "consolation" in "laboring in a cause, which has my whole heart. . . . I know it is the greatest of earthly causes. It is a part of my religion that it must prevail." Not only the impulse and the language, but the style as well was evangelical. For the educational revivalists saw their mission as converting the populace, if need be town by town, to the cause of salvation through the common school. "When I took my circuit last year," Mann reported to Barnard,

"I mounted *on top of a horse*, and went Paul Prying all along the way, and diverging off to the right or left, wherever I scented any improvement. I believe that was substantially the way that Peter the Hermit got up the Crusades."

The educational revivalists retained from their religious counterparts the evangelical ideal of a moral and spiritual regeneration of American society through the moral and spiritual regeneration of individual personalities. It is this goal that lay at the center of the new, soft, child-centered pedagogy. It was to be a pedagogy that recognized the sterility and even the danger of cold, purely intellectual education. Warning that dire consequences would result "unless the heart be so influenced in the tenderness of its young growth, that goodness becomes part of its nature," one superintendent reminded his constituents that "heart-culture should be paramount to brain-culture, moral culture to intellectual culture." Like evangelical religion, education had to awaken and shape the affective side of personality by delicately stimulating and cultivating the emotions. Like evangelism in religion as well, education thus had to engage the interest and affections of the child if it was to engender a deep, personal commitment to a righteous life.

That commitment was too important, too bound up with the future of society, to be left to chance. Consequently, schooling had to be universal, and compulsory education followed inexorably upon the demise of democratic localism. From one direction, abridgment of the freedom of property-owners by compulsory taxation for school support forecast elimination of the freedom to be unschooled. "The power which compels the citizen to pay his annual tax for the support of schools," reasoned the state superintendent in Maine, "should, in like manner, fill the schools with all of those for whose benefit the contribution was made." Taxation represented a "solemn compact between the citizen and State"; the citizen contributed in order to protect his "person" and secure his "property." The "State compelling such contributions, is under reciprocal obligation" to compel attendance at schools. Thus compulsory education became "a duty to the taxpayer."

Proponents of bureaucracy argued that the heightened importance of education in urban society required a vast increase in the proportion of community resources devoted to schooling and the attendance of all children. At first schoolmen overlooked the logic of their perception of the poor, or they might have predicted a less than enthusiastic welcome for their reformed school systems. Instead, they expected that the poor, along with everyone else, would react with warm approval to the excellence and transparent utility of new or refurbished institutions. But only the middle classes responded with enthusiasm and regularity. School promoters tried a number of expedients to promote attendance, the most notable of which was the creation of reform schools, special compulsory institutions to mop up the residue left by the regular public schools. "For those who will avail themselves of our schools, open to every child, provision is already made," wrote a Massachusetts legislative commission in 1847. "But for those who, blind to their own interests, choose the school of vicious associates only, the State has yet to provide a compulsory school, as a substitute for the prison—it may be for the gallows." The Massachusetts Reform School at Westboro, opened the following year, represented the first form of compulsory schooling in the United States.

It soon became apparent that the reform school was too small to accommodate all those who were reluctant to attend the common schools. Nor did the various truant schools in individual towns and cities solve the problem. Thus, in 1851 Massachusetts passed the first general compulsory-education law. A serious confrontation with the realities of nonattendance in that state and others had forced school promoters to recognize the logic of their long-standing position. The Pennsylvania Board of State Charities, as an instance, came to the advocacy of compulsory education by uniting the traditional relation between ignorance and crime with equally familiar arguments about the nature of cities and city children:

> The character of great cities exerts a powerful, and often a sadly controlling influence on the country, near and remote. They may be fountains of blessing to a State, or they may be sources of wide-spread corruption, nests of iniquity, festering sores upon the body politic. The children that grow up neglected in the city do not always remain there. They may carry the pestilential influence of their vices all over the State.

Reinforcing this grave danger was the unmistakable fact that "it is precisely those children whose parents or guardians are unable or indisposed to provide them with an education . . . for whom the State is most interested to provide and secure it." It was, moreover, those children who preferred "the pleasures and license of vagabondage and truancy" for whom "education is most needed." "Clearly," reasoned the board, "it is the duty, that is, it is the highest interest of the State, to secure the education of these 'neglected children,'" and the only way to accomplish this was through compulsion.

Both compulsory education and the imposition of bureaucratic reform upon reluctant communities rested on an assumption contrary to the one at the heart of democratic localism. That became perfectly clear, for example, when Thaddeus Stevens asked the delegates to the Pennsylvania Constitutional Convention of 1837: "When statesmen come into this hall, do they suppose that they come only for the purpose of acting out the ignorance of those who sent them?" If elected by men opposed to education, must a representative "therefore set his foot down against all education"? Similarly, another delegate argued, "We were told that it was dangerous to force this system upon the people, when they are not prepared to receive it; but we never heard in any state, of the people asking for provisions on the subject of education, until they were offered." The assumption here is clear: Social change flows from the top down—always and inevitably. The function of government is to lead and to educate, not to acquiesce in public whims.

That assumption made it possible to unite a number of strands and point them in only one direction. If everyone was taxed for school support, if this was justified by the necessity of schooling for the preservation of urban social order, if the beneficial impact of schooling required the regular and prolonged attendance of *all* children, and, finally, if persuasion and a variety of experiments had failed to bring all the children into school—then, clearly, education had to be compulsory. In the crunch, social change would be imposed.

Bureaucracy retained a legacy from the organizational models that it superseded. It bowed in the direction of the democrats by accepting their redefinition of voluntarism and consequently placing educational institutions under boards that were publicly elected rather than self-perpetuating. It innovated in its rejection of a loose, personalistic style of operation in favor of organizational rationality, impersonality, and professionalism. Nevertheless, in two respects the path from paternalistic voluntarism is direct. First, bureaucracy retained the notion of a central monopoly and systematized its operation through the creation of elaborately structured schools and school systems. Second, bureaucracy continued, and even strengthened, the notion that education was something the better part of the community did to the others to make them orderly, moral, and tractable. Unfortunately, the embodiment of that idea in compulsory, bureaucratic monopolies has continued to characterize American education.

Four Models: A Comparison

Thus far I have presented distinct examples of each model. This should not obscure the fact that many organizations had features of more than one, although in most instances of overlap the characteristics of a single model predominated and provided the tone. Take as one example the Boston Primary School Committee. Until 1818 Boston had only public grammar schools, entrance to which required literacy, usually acquired in small, private, fee-charging schools; this, of course, proved a burden on the poor. In 1818, after prolonged agitation, the city established a network of very small primary schools in local neighborhoods. To manage them, the city school committee itself appointed a primary-school committee, which was composed of a trustee for each school. After its initial appointment, the primary-school committee filled vacancies in its own ranks and thus became virtually self-perpetuating. Although the committee operated under public auspices, it nevertheless represents paternalistic voluntarism, because it regarded public primary education as a charity offered to the poor through the benevolent spirit and labor of an upper class.

Another sort of overlap has contaminated the bureaucratic model: the retention of democratic localism in the form of locally elected school boards, which have continued to hold ultimate authority over fully developed bureaucracies. Whether a given locality is more democratic or more bureaucratic depends on its size. In smaller communities, direct board involvement with the schools is easier, whereas in large cities the very scale of the operation, by preventing intimate board involvement, fosters bureaucratic control at all levels. It is one of the paradoxes of American education that democratic localism remains—even within cities—the official administrative ideology, while bureaucracy remains the practice.

Not all advocates of democratic localism have accepted that model in its entirety. The feature that has encouraged the most deviation has been antiprofessionalism. Democratic localists in most places were forced to recognize the appalling quality of teaching and, despite their ideological preference, realized the need to develop professional teacher training.

Finally, on occasion proponents of bureaucracy promoted corporate voluntarism. They did so in the case of public institutions that served the entire state, or a large segment of it, rather than a single community—for instance, reform schools and normal schools. In Massachusetts, philanthropists offered money to the legislature for the establishment of reform and normal schools on the condition that the grant be matched from public funds. This act, essentially a form of endowment, stimulated the state to action in the areas of both teacher training and juvenile delinquency. Both the normal school and the reform school began with their own boards of trustees, appointed by the governor. The corporate-voluntarist tone of state activity in these areas was underlined by the appointment of a separate board of trustees for each new reform and normal school created, rather than their governance by one central body.

The precise differences among the models emerge in summary fashion if we focus briefly on the four objective dimensions—scale, control, professionalism, and finance—and compare positions on each. As for scale, both the democratic localists and the corporate voluntarists advocated smallness and held the best administrative unit to be the individual institution or, at most, a section of a town. The other two models, of course, stressed size in their definition of administrative area and recommended the entire town or city, at the least, the whole state desirably, and, in some cases, the nation. On the other hand, the two varieties of voluntarist united on the question of control, favoring essentially amateur management by boards removed from direct public surveillance. On the same question, the democrats and bureaucrats united in stressing the importance of assigning management to bodies directly responsible to, and representative of, the public. However, the bureaucrats extended this position to advocate that those public bodies delegate executive responsibility to public professionals, a proposal the democrats regarded with horror.

Neither variety of voluntarist was very much concerned with the question of professionalism. Both paternalists and corporatists assumed that, as talented, educated amateurs, they were fit to manage educational institutions. Thus, when they were in control, the question of professionalism simply did not arise. Where the democrats were indifferent, interestingly, was on the question of finance. They did not especially care whether schools were absolutely free and tax-supported or partly supported by rates (a kind of fee). In fact, if free schools meant the imposition of state authority against community will, they were absolutely opposed (as the Pennsylvania constitutional convention clearly showed). The point is that free schools, while ultimately desirable, remained subordinate on the democratic-localist scale of priorities to community self-determination. The bureaucrats, with a few notable exceptions, ardently championed free schools, which were logically necessary to their ideal of universal education. The voluntarists supported tuition for those who could pay, free education for the poor, and endowment where possible.

On the question of the social role of education, the intellectual spokesmen for corporate voluntarists and democrats retained a pluralistic and sometimes libertarian vision. As one democrat put the matter, government had as a "right no control over our opinions, literary, moral, political, philosophical, or religious." To the contrary, its task was "to reflect, not to lead, nor to create the general will." Government thus "must not be installed as the educator of the people." The democrats could see no particular virtue in uniformity. It was, after all, the same writer said, the idiosyncratic character of community schools, shaped by local parents, that gave the common school its "charm."

The paternalistic voluntarists and the bureaucrats, of course, saw education in precisely the reverse light—as leading, not reflecting, the general will and at the least shaping moral opinions. The "charm" of the common school did not especially concern them, if indeed they ever noticed it. Basically, they hoped for increasing standardization of institutions, practices, and culture in American society. Safety of property, upright behavior, a reduction in crime and welfare expenses—these values marked both paternalists and bureaucrats as the advocates of law and order of their day. As an astute critic of the Massachusetts Board of Education pointed out with unmerciful clarity, the board viewed education as "merely a branch of the general police" and schoolmasters as only a "better sort of constable." The "respectable" members of the board promoted universal education "because they esteem it the most effectual means possible of checking pauperism and crime, and making the rich secure in their possessions." Education thus had "a certain utility" whose measure was "solid cash saved to the Commonwealth."

Organizational Form and Social Structure

Even if the specific models proposed in this chapter are rejected, it is my hope that the underlying argument has been persuasive. That argument is that the analysis of organizational models provides direct insight into the key value conflicts of nineteenth-century society. In their arguments over the details of organizations, nineteenth-century Americans revealed most clearly their aspirations and their anxieties concerning the society that they would build and bequeath. However, if we accept the centrality of organizational form to nineteenth-century people, we are left with an important general question: Why has the nature of organization been of such primary importance? Was it as passionate and value-laden a subject of controversy in other countries during the same period? I suspect that the answer is, at least insofar as England and Canada are concerned, not quite; Americans made organization uniquely their own *national* problem. And they did so precisely because they lacked fixed traditions and the security of ancient forms. The search for the distinctively American in art, architecture, and government, to name but three aspects of American culture, is too well known to belabor. This nervous self-consciousness knew few boundaries; it made the creation of organizations—their forms and characteristics—an intellectual and even nationalistic issue. It thus assumed special importance in the American context.

But the question of the centrality of organization can be put in a more general context as well. Even if not quite so emotionally charged, it nevertheless was important elsewhere during the nineteenth century. In both England and Canada, for instance, problems of devising or revising institutions to cope with poverty, ignorance, and other forms of social distress enlisted enormous thought and energy in precisely the same period. The explanation of that fact requires the formulation of relationships between organizations and other key aspects of nineteenth-century society, a task outside my scope in any detailed sense. However, it is important to speculate, even briefly, on the nature of that relationship and hence on the direction the inquiry into its delineation might assume. Tentatively, therefore, I should like to advance the proposition that the importance of organization derived from its mediating position between social structure and social change.

The mediating position of organizations becomes evident from a consideration of the three broad areas that must be included in any comprehensive analysis of the nineteenth century. The first is social change, perhaps best described as industrialization and urbanization. Of the three areas, that is the one we know most about. Second are changes in social structure and demographic characteristics. We have some idea of the change in the ethnic composition of the population, of its physical distribution, of the white birth rate. We know very little, in an empirical sense, about changes in structure, particularly in the family or patterns of stratification and mobility, although a number of scholars are working on these topics. However, we can be certain that there were some changes of a fairly substantial nature, whatever they may turn out to be precisely. The third area of change is organizational, which I have sketched with regard to education in this chapter.

We can observe some relations among the three major areas of change already. Paternalistic voluntarism was the form of organization characteristic of education in the preindustrial, mercantile city. Corporate voluntarism and democratic localism characterized rural areas and were proposed for urban places precisely at times of transition between mercantile and industrial stages of development. Incipient bureaucracy spread with incipient industrialization. In terms of social structure, we might suggest that paternalistic voluntarism characterized a society in which stratification was based on traditional notions of rank and deference, rather than on class in the more modern sense. Some evidence indicates that the poor and the working classes threatened by industrialization supported democratic localism in times of technological transition. However, the attempt by the middle classes to secure advantage for their children as technological change heightened the importance of formal education assured the success and acceptance of universal, elaborate, graded school systems. The same result emerged from the fear of a growing, unschooled proletariat. Education substituted for deference as a source of social cement and social order in a society stratified by class rather than by rank.

In each instance, the organization was at the center. It was the medium through which groups or classes organized their response to social imperatives. In short, organization mediated between social change and social structure. Hence men brought to the design of their organizations their values, their ambivalences, their fears, and, above all, their aspirations for the shape of American society.

Two general points about the significance of the organizational debate remain to be made. First of all, it refocuses the issue in the decreasingly profitable debate between proponents of consensus and of controversy as the key to the American past. If my underlying contention is valid, men did argue over fundamental value differences, which they articulated in reference to the practical problem of organization-building. Their interchange, the competition among organization forms, and the visions they expressed did provide a dynamic of controversy to nineteenth-century history. But it is a dynamic that implies no lack of faith in Lockean liberalism, no desire to subvert the existing social order, and no lack of commitment to America. The politics of organization-building *was* the politics of value clash, but the nature of that clash is not described by conventional categories of economic or class division. Just what those categories are—how to go beyond the empirical facts of organizational form to organized systems of values and their relationship to social structure—should be, I would argue, the major goal of American social historians.

The other point of significance regards alternatives. Men did see alternatives in the American past. Those whose vision embraced a path other than bureaucracy lost. But if the present was inevitable, it did not seem so to men at the time. Perhaps if they had been that much wiser—who can say? Their failure and their vision provide, respectively and at once, enduring notes of pessimism and hope, which we cannot afford to ignore today.

2

The Emergence of Bureaucracy in Urban Education: The Boston Case, 1850–84[*]

Educational bureaucracy did not remain incipient, as we all know. It developed quickly and thoroughly within large cities and has remained entrenched there ever since. This chapter explores the processes through which that situation came about and its consequences for reform.

The New York teachers' strike of 1968 highlighted two of those consequences for urban education. First of all, the hostility between the teachers and the various elected boards underlined the historic tension between professionals and lay reformers, between educators and the amateurs who control or try to change school systems. Second, the confrontation of teachers and angry people trying to bar them from the schools dramatized the long-standing estrangement, the distance, be-

[*] For an extended and fully documented presentation of the material in this chapter, see the two-part article that appeared under the same title in *History of Education Quarterly*, Summer, 1968, and Fall, 1968. The substance of this article is reprinted here by permission of the *History of Education Quarterly*.

tween the school and the working-class community. The two characteristics are related; both are unintended consequences of bureaucracy.

Neither was foreseen by the proponents of incipient bureaucracy. Hindsight enables us to delineate the relationship between the kind of educational structure they proposed and the tensions that characterize city school systems today. But in their eyes the problems were not inherent in the model. It was, in fact, only in practice that the weaknesses of their approach to educational reform emerged. It is therefore necessary to look closely at the context of educational reform on the local level in order to appreciate the interaction of forces that provided the dynamic of educational history and its contemporary disasters.

Bureaucracy inhibits reform. Its potent informal organizations mobilize resistance and frequently sabotage innovations. Bureaucrats counter reformist arguments by changing their own goals, replacing earlier extravagant claims with much more limited objectives, and asserting that critics misunderstand their purposes. The changes, or goal displacements, are sincerely believed in by the bureaucrats; they provide a sense of success and a buffer against tremors of self-doubt. However, in mature bureaucracies self-doubt is minimal, for the forms of organizations work changes on the personalities of those who live within them. One effect of bureaucracy is to make bureaucrats.

Bureaucracy had produced educational bureaucrats by the third quarter of the nineteenth century. That was evident in the response of schoolmen to educational critics. It was one lesson of the major controversy that rocked the Boston school system in the 1870's.

That the battle took place in Boston at that time was no accident; similar fights were being waged throughout the country at the same time. In essence, they were skirmishes between lay reformers, disenchanted with the rigid educational organizations that had so quickly emerged out of the enthusiastic educational revival of mid-century, and the now more organized and powerful schoolmen. To understand the controversy in Boston and elsewhere, it is critical to appreciate the significance of the structural alteration in the organization of urban education during the third quarter of the nineteenth century.

For the most part, histories of education follow a long-established pattern of periodization. The "revival of education" marked the few decades before the Civil War; then came "expansion of the educational enterprise," lasting from the 1870's to the 1960's, punctuated by "progressivism," which arose with reformist vigor in the 1890's and degenerated into the child-centered school by the 1920's. The trouble with this framework is that the common word "expansion" implies an evolutionary, teleological process, increments of the same piled on top of one another. Significant changes in direction are masked, and one of the most significant is the change in the nature of school systems that was effected in most areas of the East and Midwest between, roughly, 1850 and 1875. During those years, urban school systems became, in a word, bureaucracies. Except in the South, the principle of free, tax-supported public schools had been generally accepted by the time of the Civil War, but the form and organization those schools would assume in urban America had not yet been fixed. It was the function of developments in the few succeeding decades to stamp irrevocably upon urban education the classic features of bureaucracy. To examine those years, as we do in this chapter, is to explore the origins of contemporary patterns of urban educational administration and of two related major predicaments of contemporary educational reformers—the need for alternative models of educational organization, and the divorce of school and community. Besides attempting to reveal the beginnings, this chapter suggests that bureaucratization provides a valid framework for reinterpreting a number of developments and controversies in late-nineteenth-century urban education. Urban educational bureaucracies developed with local idiosyncrasies that make each unique in some ways, but they were all responses to the same kinds of pressure. Close examination of one will therefore yield more insight than a superficial recounting of many.

The Emergence of Bureaucracy

Between 1850 and 1876 the Boston school system became a full-scale bureaucracy. Bureaucracy has come to have negative connotations, perhaps rightly so, but the intent here is to use the term first of all to denote an organization marked by certain identifiable structural features. Social scientists differ concerning the exact nature of these features. The definition offered by Carl Friedrich matched the Boston situation better than the more familiar one by Max Weber; the former is more clearly stated and stems from a comparison of relatively modern political-administrative units. "The six elements of a bureaucracy," writes Friedrich, "fall naturally into two groups. Three of them order the relations of the members of the organization to each other—namely, centralization of control and supervision, differentiation of function, and qualification for office (entry and career aspects)—while three embody rules defining desirable habit or behavior patterns of all the members of such an organization—namely, objectivity, precision and consistency, and discretion." All of the elements of bureaucracy listed by Friedrich emerged in Boston during the third quarter of the nineteenth century, as Tables 1 and 2 partially reveal.

The first element of bureaucracy identified by Friedrich, "centralization of control and supervision," was reflected in the shift from a system of diffuse supervision by more than a hundred lay officials to a small school board and full-time central administrators. "Differentiation of function," the sec-

Table 1

Structure of the Boston School System, 1850 and 1876

A. Lay Supervision

1850		1876	
School committee	24 members[a]	School board	24 members[c]
Primary school committee	73 members[b]		
Total	97	Total	24

[a] Two members elected from each of the city's twelve wards in 1850, with the mayor as ex officio chairman; changed to six elected from each ward in 1854, growing to 118 members.

[b] Appointed by, but with authority independent of, the school committee; abolished in 1855, and jurisdiction transferred to school committee.

[c] As of 1875, twenty-four members elected at large from the city; name changed from committee to board that year.

B. Professional Supervision

1850		1876	
None		Superintendent	1[a]
		Board of supervisors	6 members[b]
		Principals	48[c]
		Total	55

[a] First superintendent appointed in 1851.

[b] Position of supervisor created by legislation in 1875.

[c] Masters of grammar schools appointed principals of both their own schools and primary schools in their districts in 1866.

C. Types of Schools

	1850			1876		
	Enroll-ment	No. of Schools	No. of Teachers	Enroll-ment	No. of Schools	No. of Teachers
Primary	11,000[a]	161	164	19,221	114	423
Grammar	9,071	22	167	24,788	50	580
Latin (high school)[b]	96	1	3	355	1	18
English (high school)[c]	165	1	5	483	1	20
Girls (high school)[d]	—	—	—	569	1	25
Suburban high schools[e]	—	—	—	516	5	51
Normal school[f]	—	—	—	69	1	8

Table 1 (*cont.*)

	1850			1876		
	Enroll-ment	No. of Schools	No. of Teachers	Enroll-ment	No. of Schools	No. of Teachers
School for deaf mutes[g]	—	—	—		1	8
School for licensed minors[h]	—	—	—		1	2
Kindergarten[i]	—	—	—		1	1
Evening schools[j]	—	—	—		17	142
Evening drawing schools[k]	—	—	—		4	16
Totals		185	339		197	1,294

[a] Approximate figure.

[b] Established in 1635, took students of grammar as well as high school age.

[c] Established in 1821.

[d] Separated from normal school and established in 1872.

[e] Includes Brighton High School, established in 1841; Charlestown High School, 1848; West Roxbury High School, 1849; Roxbury High School, 1852; Dorchester High School, 1852. All came into Boston system as a result of annexation of respective towns.

[f] Established in 1852.

[g] Established in 1869.

[h] Established in 1867. A licensed minor was a newsboy.

[i] Established in 1870.

[j] Evening schools established in 1857, and evening high school in 1869.

[k] Established in 1870.

Note: Figures mask an internal change: Primary schools were not only consolidated and made larger but also graded, starting in 1857. Grading of grammar schools began in 1847.

D. Special Instructors[a]

1850	1876	
None	General supervisor of music	1
	Director of music	6
	Normal art instructor and general supervisor of drawing	1
	Special instructor in drawing	6
	Vocal and physical culture, high school	1
	Military drill, high school	1
	French, high school	5
	German, high school	3
	Sewing, grammar school[b]	26
	Truant officers	14

[a] Special instructors are also included in numbers of teachers in part C.

[b] Authorization to teach sewing given in 1854.

Table 1 (*cont.*)

E. School Expenditures

	1850	1876
Total	$311,494.95	$15,252,199.73
Per pupil	$10.65	$29.88
Tax rate[a]	.00092	.00186

[a] Amount per dollar of assessed valuation raised by taxes for school support.

F. Population

	1850	1876
Total	138,788	341,919
Ages 5–15	24,275	66,720

Table 2

Hierarchy of Teaching Positions and Salaries

	1850	1876
High school teachers, male	Ranks: master, submaster Latin school, submaster English school, usher	Termed first-grade teachers. Ranks: headmaster, master, submaster, usher
	Salary range: $800–2,400 ($1,320–3,750)[a]	Salary range: $1,700–4,000, including increments within each position
High school teachers, female	None	Termed third-grade teachers. Ranks: assistant principal; first, second, third, and fourth assistants; normal-school assistant
		Salary range: $1,000–2,000
Grammar school teachers, male	Ranks: grammar and writing, master, usher	Termed second-grade teachers. Ranks: masters, submasters, ushers
	Salary range: $300–1,500 ($490–2,960)	Salary range: $1,700–3,200, including increments within each position
Grammar school teachers, female	(Salary of grammar school teachers not differentiated by sex; most likely all those labeled assistant were female)	Termed fourth-grade teachers. Ranks: first, second, and third assistants

Table 2 (*cont.*)

	1850	1876
		Salary range: $600–1,200, with increments only for third assistants
Primary school teachers	Primary school teacher	Termed fifth-grade teachers. Rank: fourth assistant
	Salary: $300 ($490)	Salary range: $600–800
Special teachers	None	Termed special grade teachers. 36 different positions, e.g., director of drawing, music
		Top salary: $3,300
Supervisory personnel	None	Three types: superintendent, $4,500; supervisor, $4,000; principal, paid according to teaching rank held.

a Figures in parentheses indicate approximate value of 1850 salaries adjusted for changes in cost of living to 1876 equivalents.

ond element in Friedrich's definition, was also apparent in both ways he has used the term. First, technical differentiation occurred as administrative duties became fixed and defined by regulation and as departments, specialist teachers, specialized schools, and age-grading were introduced. The practice of requiring all teachers to teach all subjects altered with the emergence of a whole corps of specialist instructors, most of whom traveled between two or more schools, teaching only their specialty. The second sort of differentiation, the development of hierarchy, emerged as the number of ranks within the system expanded and the salary gap between the highest and lowest positions widened.

The third element of bureaucracy is "qualification for office"—that is, appointment and promotion on the basis of objective qualifications. In 1850 the loose rules for the examination of teachers were applied casually, and the examinations themselves were conducted by amateurs whose capacity for determining the fitness of a candidate for teaching was undetermined. The teachers themselves, by and large, had had no specific pedagogical training. By 1876 the level of appointment of a teacher supposedly rested on predetermined, professionally derived and administered standards; examinations, now much more formal, were conducted by the supervisors, and which of the different classes of certificates was awarded to the candidates depended on their performance on the tests. A sizable proportion of teachers, moreover, now had been trained in normal schools, especially the one operated by the city.

The Boston school system for the most part reflected the behavioral as well as the organizational elements of bureaucracy. One such behavioral element is "objectivity" or "expertise" in performance. Innovations and administrative decisions had traditionally been made by amateur lay officials without professional advice or opinions. By 1876 an increasing number of decisions were being left to the career administrators, and, with some notable exceptions, the career administrators (considered "experts") exerted more and more influence on the decisions of the school board itself.

"Precision and consistency" constitute a second behavioral aspect of bureaucracy. Only meager statistics were gathered in 1850; there was no set pattern for administrative routine; the whims and preferences of lay officials largely governed their administrative and supervisory actions, which consequently had little consistency. By 1876 the gathering of elaborate statistics to serve as a basis for analysis and decision-making had become an established custom; rules existed to routinize administrative decisions and introduce consistency. In one respect, however, the Boston school system did not reflect this element of bureaucracy, for, despite the complaints of schoolmen and their supporters, there was no tenure system to assure continuity of personnel, and both administrators and teachers remained quite insecure.

The final element of bureaucratic behavior is "discretion."

No secret or private information was gathered in Boston in 1850; in 1876, however, the supervisors introduced a "black book," in which they recorded judgments on individual teachers. The book, which became infamous among the teachers, was open only to the school board and superintendent.

The bureaucratization of the Boston school system between 1850 and 1876 illustrated a general process taking place in other aspects of American urban life. In Boston, for instance, the various functions originally associated with the police were gradually being assigned to new, specialized agencies, and the police force itself was becoming professionalized and more elaborate in organization. The bureaucratization of urban education elsewhere was made clear by commentators who tried to describe American education in the 1870's and 1880's. Take, as an example, the critical description by Burke A. Hinsdale, then President of Hiram College in Ohio:

> Our common schools constitute a highly complex and differentiated, a vast and powerful system. The machinery of this system is tens of thousands of school houses, thousands of libraries, vast illustrative apparatus, boards of directors and boards of examiners, normal schools and institutes, reports and bureaus, commissioners and superintendents, and more than a quarter of a million of teachers. In the towns and cities, the system has taken on a form especially complex and costly. There are the primary, grammar and high schools, with their grades, A, B, C, and D, not to mention the minor divisions which a layman can hardly keep in his head while hearing them; each one of which divisions is supposed to represent some definable stage in the training of a man. There are the teachers of the various grades, from the primary teachers up by way of the principal to the Superintendent of Public Instruction and his staff of assistants. Behind these come trooping in the kindergarten teachers, the normal and training teachers, followed by the music and drawing masters—each one having his bundle of reports under his arm and his sheet of percentages in his hand. The whole body of public school teachers constitute an intelli-

gent, active and powerful profession; presenting in some respects the appearance of an hierarchy of education.

To describe the creation of bureaucracy in Boston or elsewhere, important as that task is, is not to explain why urban school systems became bureaucracies in the third quarter of the nineteenth century. From the timing of the various developments in Boston, one important fact about the nature of bureaucratization becomes clear: It did not emerge full blown. Although the structural features of the Boston school system were clearly interrelated, they had developed singly and at different times. In this sense "bureaucratization" can be a somewhat misleading term, unless one realizes that it is being used to encompass a number of distinct innovations and alterations, such as age-grading, the introduction of a superintendent, and the centralization of the school board. Bureaucratization, that is, was a piecemeal process. Thus, an account of the reasons for each structural change is necessary in order to explain the development of bureaucracy. However, a more general approach to the problem is still possible, because underlying the different innovations were certain pressures and predicaments that forced educational development in the direction of bureaucracy.

Perhaps the most fundamental problem facing school systems was the increasing complexity of the task of administering urban education. For example, in 1855 the city of Boston had only a superintendent and a school committee of seventy-six part-time lay members to supervise and coordinate more than 160 primary schools, which fed nearly fifty grammar schools that led, in turn, to the two high schools. As a part-time pursuit of busy people, the school committee could not oversee the work of individual schools with any care. Under the recently abolished primary school committee, at least someone had been responsible for each school. In some cases this undoubtedly led to close if paternalistic supervision. Now, however, the schools, taught by largely untrained young girls chosen by haphazard methods, were left without guidance. The superintendent, for all his remarkable energy, certainly could not regularly visit and advise more than 200 schools. Thus, there was little coordination or direction in the school system, which was staggering under an increasingly crowded and heterogeneous population. Grammar school masters had no assurance that the children coming to them from the primary schools had received a reasonably systematic, competently taught primary education. Nor, on the other hand, could the high schools be certain that their students had a reasonably common educational background. No reliable or systematic process existed for weeding out ineffectual teachers or for preventing their entry into the system at the primary level. In short, it was argued, to function with any degree of efficiency and effectiveness the school system desperately needed some coordination and increased supervision. In 1851 that line of argument had been effective in persuading the school committee to hire the first superintendent; it was convincing in 1876 in spurring the appointment of a board of supervisors and in streamlining the school committee. The argument was effective, too, in making the grammar school masters principals of the primary schools in their districts.

The complexity of administration was an implicit assumption in the educational ideal of urban superintendents throughout the country, who argued that all large organizations, from industry to the army, depended for coordination on centralized professional direction by a superintending officer. The success of professional supervision, especially in the various branches of industry, indicated the need for the same type of direction in education. Supervision was deemed necessary because organizations had to be based on division of labor, which, to these superintendents, was the process underlying social development. According to the influential superintendent and professor of pedagogy William H. Payne, the growth of civilization represented "a process of differentiation," whose stages of progress could be measured by the degree of functional separation between activities. Differentiation within school systems was thus an integral and progressive part of the development of a more civilized and complex society. And this differentiation introduced a need for specialization and coordination not present in earlier periods. Underlying the belief in the necessity of division of labor in school management was the assumption that the growing size and expanded role of the schools had made their management a far more difficult and specialized task than it had been. Thus, schoolmen saw such innovations as the superintendency, the elaboration of hierarchy, and specialization as necessary ways of meeting their increasingly complex tasks.

Schoolmen over and over again used the example of industry as an idealized standard that formed the basis for their justifications of the superintendency. They often described their school systems as factories and used metaphors based on the corporation and the machine. Modern industry, they could see, had developed its remarkable capacity through a rational organization that stressed hierarchy, the division of labor, and intensive professional supervision. If those methods worked in industries as diverse as textiles and railroads, why would they not work in education? Still, it is unlikely that schoolmen attempted to model their systems directly on factories. They never advocated so minute a division of labor, for instance, nor did they ask for quite so much passivity in their teachers, as supervisors of factories required of their workers. An intensive comparative analysis of school and factory organization in the period has yet to be made, but it is likely that such an analysis would find that schoolmen used the industrial analogy loosely, to justify the introduction and elaboration of certain general features of their school systems, such as supervision and departmentalization. This supposition is reinforced by the very vagueness with which industrial analogies were employed. No superintendent made a close study of the structure of industry or bothered to discriminate between service and production industries. Nor did any of them see any inconsistency in switching from an industrial analogy to a military one. Rather, the success of industry highlighted the relevance to schools of certain general features of organizations because both factory and school superintendent were faced with the same underlying problem: the coordination of large numbers of people in a complex enterprise. Because industry had seemingly conquered the problem of coordination, it offered valuable lessons for public education.

Schoolmen pointed out that a professionally supervised school system based on the division of labor should ideally have certain structural features and that its participants should have certain attitudes. An elaborate hierarchical structure and an explicit chain of command were necessary to keep each member working at his particular task in a responsible and coordinated fashion. At the head of the hierarchy should be one "vested with sufficient authority" to "devise plans in general and in detail" and to "keep all subordinates in their proper places and at their assigned tasks." Within the hierarchy, moreover, roles and duties should be defined clearly to avoid the possibility of conflict, and all members should give unquestioning, prompt obedience to the orders of their superiors. The great danger in a complex organization, according to Payne, was "disintegration," caused chiefly by "nonconformity," something not to be tolerated in either pupils or teachers.

To perfect their hierarchies, schoolmen argued, it was necessary to carry the development of career lines within school systems even further. If education was to become an attractive profession to men, "promotion from the ranks" was an absolute requisite. The introduction of tenure and pensions was also needed, they asserted. Subject to annual election by a school board, superintendents and teachers were thoroughly insecure and forced into timidity for the sake of survival. Moreover, the teacher, generally paid a meager salary, was unable to save and had to teach until he was forced from the classroom by total disability or death. When all teachers were offered a career, security, and protection from arbitrary dismissal, schoolmen asserted, hierarchical systems would be nearly perfect.

Bureaucratic innovations were introduced as part of a continuing process of rationalizing and coordinating the increasingly complex urban school systems. Added to the challenge of complexity were the problems of politics and personalities. Hardly anyone at the time would have quarreled with the position that teachers should be chosen for their qualifications and not for reasons of personal favoritism or nepotism. But diffuse, lay-controlled school systems made objectivity a scarce commodity. Politics exacerbated the situation, for to anchor school boards to city wards was to put them in the midst of the most intense political pressures, with often predictable results. Features of bureaucracy designed to provide impartial standards and centralize control were defenses against favoritism. The introduction of supervisors in Boston, for instance, was considered a means of lifting the appointment of teachers above the personal, amateur, and political level, since the supervisors conducted examinations for training positions. The development of more elaborate and specific written regulations was intended to make the operation of the school system more routine—that is, more impartial and equitable—and the removal of the school board from ward politics was designed to remove the schools from partisanship as well as to foster increased coordination through centralization.

Another reason for the development of bureaucracy is critical: It offered specific advantages to practicing schoolmen in their quest for "professionalism." It therefore enlisted their wholehearted and vigorous support. The first of these advantages we have already noted: the development of career lines within education. Superintendents fostering the elaboration of hierarchies were really creating careers for themselves and their contemporaries. Partly, their motivation was undoubtedly altruistic: a desire to create conditions that would attract more able men into education. Partly, too, they no doubt wished to improve their own chances of advancement; those who had reached top positions could see in hierarchy an augmenting of their own power, as armies of subordinates became increasingly subject to their control.

Bureaucratization also served schoolmen by mitigating an emerging problem: the regulation of behavior within the occupation itself. The concern of schoolmen with this issue was disclosed by Thomas Bicknell, in a presidential address to the National Council of Education. Bicknell noted that the alluring prospect of a rapidly ascending career was tempting ambitious individuals and often introducing into school systems destructive careerist competition that generated hostility and tension among an entire staff. The division of educational opinion in the country offered "perpetual temptation" to "undignified intrigue" and "violent excitement." The newly formed Council, composed of the elite of practicing American educators, would serve as a "warning to ambitious young teachers" by offering authoritative pronouncements on the bewildering array of innovations being peddled around the country. Most likely, schoolmen hoped that the Council would reinforce on a national level the sort of regulation of behavior that bureaucracies were trying to enforce on a local level. Bureaucracy places a premium on acquiescent, rule-following behavior. In this type of organization the individualist, the aggressively ambitious, is not only uncomfortable but unacceptable. The instruments that educational bureaucrats had for regulating behavior were uniform rules and prescribed patterns of action (such as centrally defined courses of study), coupled with the sanctions of colleagueship and promotion obtainable only for faithful service and quiet good behavior.

Schoolmen undoubtedly hoped to reduce the tension and the threat to themselves that arose from eccentric and innovative behavior on the part of such mavericks as the superintendent of Quincy, Mass., Francis Parker.

Thus, in the third quarter of the nineteenth century, increasingly complex administrative problems, reinforced by the nepotism and politics that afflicted school practice, made rationalization and coordination a necessity for urban school systems. Faced with this need, schoolmen (and some laymen as well) justified their organizing principles by analogies from industry, which they believed had successfully solved the same basic problem: the management of large numbers of people performing different tasks. The process of bureaucratization within education was so thorough and so rapid because of the enthusiasm of the schoolmen themselves, who saw in the new organizational forms the opening up of careers and a partial solution to the problem of regulating behavior within the occupation.

The schoolmen's ability to foster the development of hierarchical differentiated systems as rapidly as they did was due to another important factor: They met little opposition. One reason was that in the beginning influential laymen agreed with their goals. Bureaucracy, as we have observed, represented a crystallization of bourgeois social values. Besides, particular innovations in the direction of bureaucracy often gave differential advantage to the children of the affluent. Complementing that fact, the years of the rapid spread of bureaucracy were precisely the years of withdrawal of lay interest in education. By the mid-1850's, the first enthusiastic phase of the ante bellum educational revival had begun to decline, and the lay interest that had sustained the movement dwindled. The ante bellum reformers, however, had planted the seeds of bureaucracy by fostering an increase in the number of common schools and teachers, by urging grading, and by sponsoring the development of high schools. They had, moreover, called into being the first professional administrators, the superintendents, to help them with the management of these rather sprawling and uncoordinated systems. As lay interest lessened, the new class of professional educators consolidated the systems they had inherited. For roughly two decades, schoolmen were able to carry on the task of consolidation with a minimum of lay interference. In the process they introduced into the new school systems the features of bureaucracy that I have been examining. The withdrawal of lay zeal had left school systems open to capture by the professionals, who, quickly perceiving the advantages of bureaucracy, had acted with dispatch to build large, hierarchical, differentiated, uniform, and rigid organizations.

Critics of Education: The New School Board vs. John Dudley Philbrick

In the 1870's, a wave of criticism of the public schools spread throughout the country. Critics aimed their attacks at the results of public education, at its bureaucratic structure, and, especially in the beginning, at its costs. As citizens around the country searched for means of trimming municipal expenses in the aftermath of the depression of 1873, they turned their attention to the schools with an intensity that generally had been lacking for nearly two decades, and they noted with alarm that expenditures for public education had mounted enormously since the 1850's. Indeed, although financing remained far from adequate, one of the successes of the new class of career administrators had been in persuading the public to spend steadily increasing amounts of money on their schools. When laymen turned to the schools with renewed attention in the hope of cutting costs, they discovered to their horror that the quality of education was dreadfully low and, so they said, had actually declined. By 1875 the sentiment of community leaders in Boston, reflecting national criticism of public education, clearly favored a radical reform in the school system. The editor of the *Transcript*, for one, observed that "grave doubts are creeping about as to the absolute perfection claimed and conceded for the school system. . . . The system is, first, too costly, and next, too vital if it cost nothing, to escape criticism much longer."

Aside from the desire to cut expenses, reformers, at the start of their campaign, would have found it hard to express their goals precisely. The concrete aims of the reformist movement emerged, as we shall see, in the course of its development. In the beginning, reformers seemed to feel that something was wrong with the schools: Children learned too little and that not well; the atmosphere of the schools was too rigid and mechanical; the key personnel of the system exerted too strong a hold on its operation. Fresh thinking was imperative.

The first actions of the would-be reformers were contradictory. Their initial achievement was to obtain from the state legislature a bill calling for the appointment of supervisors by the school board and reducing the board from 118 members elected from wards to 24 elected at large. On the one hand, this action represented an attempt to continue the trend toward centralization of power and increased expertise in administration, classic aspects of bureaucratization that had marked educational development in Boston for twenty-five years. But the reformers were also concerned to change the operation of the system itself and to break the hold of the existing leaders. Because they felt considerable contempt for the career personnel of the schools, they went about their attempt to improve the system in a way that deliberately undercut the authority of the superintendents by failing to define and demarcate clearly the duties and spheres of influence of the supervisors, the new addition to the hierarchy. Thus the reformers' actions contradicted their professed ideal of rational, centralized organization. The immediate result was an ambiguity of role definition for administrators within the system and, hence, a vicious conflict that effectively prevented the new administrative arrangements from doing much good.

Opponents of the measure pointed out that the motivation behind the legislation changing the nature of school administration appeared to be more complex than a simple effort to bring about reform through centralization. Most of the opposition came from Catholics who believed the maneuver was intended to exclude them from the management of school affairs. They asserted, too, that the bill had been pushed through the school committee in an illegal and clandestine manner. Of course, no supporters of the legislation ever openly admitted to any anti-Catholic sentiment, although that may well have been part of their motivation. They based their case, and it was a good one, on the inefficiency of a large board, the preponderance of unqualified members, and the danger that partisan politics and even corruption might enter school affairs conducted at the ward level.

Leading citizens in Boston, like their counterparts elsewhere, were searching for a way of overcoming the partisanship and corruption that had entered the political life of the expanding city. While the reorganization of the school committee was being proposed, the legislature was considering (and ultimately rejected) a new city charter designed to mitigate partisan politics in city affairs by increasing the power of intelligent and disinterested public executives. Parallel efforts were under way in other places. For instance, accompanying the introduction of the superintendency in the town of Quincy was a change in the method of the town meeting, designed to remove essential decisions from the mass of the participants; accompanying the reorganization of the school committee in Boston was an attempt to change the nature of city government; in both places, municipal and educational reforms were part of a program for overcoming the weaknesses of urban democracy. Here is where, in a modified form, the charges of the Catholics probably had some validity. Mugwumps like Charles Francis Adams, Jr., who sponsored the reform in Quincy, held the immigrants and their spokesmen responsible for a decline in the quality of municipal life; consequently, attempts to reform civic conduct were, by definition, efforts to reduce the power of the newcomers.

The first important task of the streamlined Boston school board was to elect a superintendent, for in the middle of 1874 John Dudley Philbrick, who had been superintendent since 1856, had resigned. Philbrick was an important man in educational circles that extended beyond Boston. The editor of the *New England Journal of Education* called him "a representative American educator," and the phrase was quite accurate. At one time or another, Philbrick was president of almost every important state and national educational association. He was far more than a local superintendent; he was one of the few recognized spokesmen for American schoolmen. One reason for Philbrick's resignation, offered in retrospect, was ill health, but it is likely that he sensed the impending change in school organization and wanted to give the new board a chance to start afresh with a new superintendent. That the new board might want a different superintendent he had good reason to believe, because the growing public dissatisfaction with the schools reflected more than a little on his management. Although the representative of the schoolmen's interests in Boston, the *New England Journal of Education*, expected that Philbrick would be chosen again, his candidacy ran into serious trouble as a faction of the school board, in a surprise move, tried to elect someone else to the superintendency. Philbrick was re-elected despite the opposition, but his position as superintendent, with a goodly portion of his aggressively reformist school board against him, was shaky, to say the least.

After choosing a superintendent, the board had to elect six people to fill the newly created, important, and highly paid ($4,000 a year) positions of supervisors. The duties of the supervisors were far from clear. The act that had established the school board merely stated that six supervisors should be appointed, leaving the definition of their duties to the board. Together with the superintendent as chairman, the six supervisors formed the board of supervisors; they were left virtually free to develop examinations and to organize the way in which they would carry out their other assignments.

Here it is critical to note that the line between the duties of the supervisors and those of the superintendent was far from clear. The school board had created an imperfect hierarchy whose top members had overlapping authority and duties, a situation bound to breed trouble. The potential for conflict was increased by the nature of the appointments themselves. A committee of the school board nominated twelve people as supervisors, of whom the first six in order of preference were practicing schoolmen. Had those six been elected, much of the trouble that ensued would have been avoided, for they and Philbrick would have shared common assumptions about their respective duties and authority and about the management of urban schools.

The reform faction within both school board and city was not satisfied; when the balloting was over, only two of the committee's first choices had been elected. The remaining four new supervisors were men with little practical experience in public education. The majority of the supervisors, in short, represented the lay reformist interest on the school board. The result of the school board's inconsistency was predictable: By electing both Philbrick, a schoolman of known views and temperament, and a majority of supervisors representing lay reformist interests, people whose views would conflict with his, the board set the stage for the debilitating quarrel that rocked Boston's schools during the next eight years.

Throughout the first year under the new arrangement, the conflict between the board of supervisors and the superintendent simmered just barely below the surface. By the end of the year it had come into full public view. It was, of course, not only Philbrick who looked with some suspicion at the new board; the grammar and high school masters liked it no better. The teachers knew of the secrecy involved in the supervisors' operations; they were rated by the "supervisors according to a numerical scale in a book open not for our inspection but to the inspection of the committee." They realized that their "work was reported on and . . . defects noted in another book, also open to the committee but not to us." Therefore, the teachers regarded supervision as a "euphemistic term for espionage. There was a widespread prejudice against it. Although hostile to the supervisors, the teachers did not complain publicly, for their position was painfully tenuous. Each year they faced re-election by the school board, and public criticism of school policy could easily cost an experienced teacher his job. Complained one commentator, "It is a notorious fact that the mouths of our teachers are closed."

Philbrick acted with surprising force to discredit the work of the supervisors. In a section of his semiannual report entitled "The New Departure," he attacked the plan of work adopted by the supervisors. So incensed was the school board by his action that it forced him to expurgate the report. Although the officially published document did not contain Philbrick's accusations, he nevertheless published the original version of his report separately and reprinted the offending section in the *New England Journal of Education*.

The school board itself moved more and more toward the side of the supervisors. Because of the intense and now public controversy, two subcommittees were appointed to investigate the relationship between superintendent and supervisors. The first offered, in vague language, an unconvincing elaboration of the supervisors' point of view and an exoneration of the regulations governing their actions. The second, instead of offering substantive motions, tried to analyze the source of the friction; its only contribution was the pious hope that the two sides could settle their differences peacefully. Philbrick himself showed a desire to moderate the conflict. For some time he had held monthly meetings of the grammar and high school masters, and at one of these in 1876 he had described the reasons for the reorganization of the school committee and asked the masters for cooperation.

Philbrick's attempt to reach a compromise with the supervisors failed. As the reformist influence on the school board grew more dominant, his position progressively worsened. By January, 1878, the time for the next election of a superintendent, his fate was clear. After twenty-two years of hard service as superintendent of schools, Philbrick was unceremoniously fired. In any event such a situation would not lack pathos, but the harshness of the act was underscored by Philbrick's "expressed desire to be vindicated by a re-election, after which he was determined to resign." Ruthlessly bent on change, the school board would not allow Philbrick the dignity of an honorable retirement.

It is hard not to sympathize with Philbrick in his quarrel with the school board. He had labored long and energetically to construct and operate a school system. He had worked without any security in a city subject to all the stresses and frustrations that accompanied late-nineteenth-century population growth and urban politics. In this trying setting he had managed not only to hang onto his job, a feat not to be taken lightly, but also to bring increasing order and system to the schools of Boston. True, he ran an expensive school system, but his plausible answer to this criticism was, first, that fewer children attended private and parochial schools in Boston than in any other large city and, second, that good schools were expensive. That the schools were good by the standards of the time is a conclusion reinforced by the reports of many foreign observers who claimed that the Boston schools were the best in the nation. But the issue was not a simple one, and virtue did not reside entirely on Philbrick's side. Philbrick

lacked imagination, vision, and the desire or instinct to innovate radically. His ideal of education was dull, mechanical,
and rigid. It is unclear just what further progress education in
Boston would have made under his continued direction, aside
from a further systematization of administration, and it is unlikely that he would have inspired the reforms in pedagogy
and tone necessary to infuse vitality into the classrooms. Insofar as the reformers had as their goal the kind of freeing of the
curriculum and change in spirit that Francis Parker effected in
nearby Quincy, they were urging innovations that were needed
by urban schools. And their perception that the existing key
people in the Boston schools, the superintendent and his lieu-
tenants, the grammar masters, would not introduce those
reforms without a hard shove from an outside source was
undoubtedly accurate. But the reformers lacked sensitivity
and a sense of strategy. They had no realistic idea of how to
effect the changes they desired, and they were totally unaware
and careless of the feelings of those they would reform, so cal-
lous that they could fire John Dudley Philbrick a few months
before he intended to retire.

The school board undoubtedly hoped that Philbrick was
sufficiently crushed to sink quietly into oblivion. But he was
not to be silenced, and he added to the bitterness aroused by
his firing by sending a long defensive letter to the *Transcript*.
Nor did the school board count on the possibility that Philbrick might rise to even greater eminence and thereby attain
a position from which he could counterattack with increased
prestige and authority. But that is what happened, for in
March, 1878, Philbrick left the superintendency of the Boston
schools to become United States Commissioner of Education
at the Paris Exposition. Temporarily he was gone from Boston, but, if the school committee breathed a sigh of relief, it
was a sigh of false optimism. The submerged anger of the
masters at Philbrick's firing made further trouble inevitable.
Philbrick, as I have noted, had promoted the interests of the

masters and increased their powers substantially. In turn he had won their loyalty. The school board had seriously under-estimated both the popularity and the strength of their oppo-nent and the resistance of his supporters. By firing Philbrick it had not quieted but instead inflamed the controversy.

The removal of Philbrick ended the first phase of the dis-pute, which had disclosed one of the problems inherent in the development of a bureaucracy—namely, the definition of roles. When bureaucracy arises in piecemeal fashion, as it did in Boston, the demarcation of duties and lines of authority becomes blurred, and tensions arising from overlapping func-tions are almost inevitable. In Boston this problem was ex-acerbated by the sloppy way in which the school board went about the process of organization-building. The board mem-bers in those years proved to be both bad bureaucrats and ineffectual reformers. Instead of rejuvenating the schools, all they did was cause trouble. Although they may have had a more lively idea of the possibilities of education than Philbrick did, they did not share his understanding of organizations and their constraints. After it had disposed of Philbrick, the re-formist faction attempted to go about its job in a more thor-ough, ruthless, and efficient manner. But, again, it ultimately failed because of its insensitivity to the nature of organization. In this case, the aspect of organization the reformers failed to reckon with was the power of entrenched informal groups within the system itself.

Critics of Bureaucracy: The Attack on the Grammar School Masters

The Boston school board added to its problems by its choice of a successor to Philbrick. Samuel Eliot (a relative of Har-vard's president) had little practical experience in the admin-istration of public education. Following his graduation from Harvard (first in his class), Eliot had toured Europe and written a series of history books. In 1856, aged 35, Eliot became Professor of History and Political Science at Trinity College, Hartford, and from 1860 to 1866 he served as Trinity's president. In 1874 (the intervening eight years are vague) he became principal of the Girls' High and Normal School in Boston but resigned the position after only two years because of ill health and family bereavement. The scholarly Eliot, near-amateur in public school affairs, appealed to the reformist element of the school board, and his reports quickly made it evident that he sympathized with the faction that had deposed Philbrick. Eliot's snobbish social Darwinism and isolation from the schools compounded his problems. As a practical administrator, he was generally inept. In contrast to Philbrick's reports, Eliot's were filled not with pragmatic discussions of practical subjects but with long and florid discourses more suited to a late-nineteenth-century literary magazine than to the reports of an urban superintendent.

Throughout 1878 the reformist faction continued to gain power. At the annual election later in the year, fourteen of the twenty-four places on the school committee passed to new people. Although one new member, former grammar school master George Hyde, was a solid schoolman, the new committee, led by Brooks Adams, was heavily reformist in composition. Adams had a model for educational reform in the experience of his older brother, Charles Francis Adams, Jr., who had been deeply involved in the school reform of nearby Quincy, the movement usually associated with Francis Parker.

Ebullient, charismatic, and a thoroughgoing individualist, Parker was described by one influential school observer as the "poet of the new elementary education." Upon his return from studying educational theory and practice in Europe, he had so captivated the school board of Quincy (including Charles Francis Adams, Jr.) that they had given him virtually complete control of school policy, with the exception of finances, and a mandate to revolutionize the town's schools. Parker justified their expectations by radically altering the curriculum, pedagogy, and tone of the Quincy schools. Through his own infectious zeal and love of children he had inspired the town's teachers to make their schools places where children's happiness was of paramount concern. Many of the thousands of observers who annually trooped to Quincy to view Parker's work, loudly advertised by the Adamses and other school board members, testified to his success. And it was not only the tone of the school that he changed. A comparative analysis of educational achievement in Quincy and elsewhere showed that, where Parker's influence had been strongest, children had actually learned to read, write, and cipher much better. At the same time Parker managed to double the enrollment of the high school, eliminate the problem of irregular attendance, and almost end truancy, feats that other Massachusetts towns and cities had been striving unsuccessfully to achieve for decades.

Boston's new school board, like Quincy's, offered a diagnosis of educational ills that reflected the concern of lay reformers throughout the country about the cost and quality of education. Added to this was their often subtle perception of the consequences of bureaucratic rigidity, in particular the effects of bureaucracy on the personalities and behavior of its members. "Many minds," wrote one critic, "are incapable of using forms without becoming their slaves." Equally unfortunate was the fact that routine and ritual drive a wedge between teacher and pupil, altering what had once been a much more vital and meaningful relationship. The "personal force of the teacher," Burke Hinsdale lamented, "goes for much less," and the pupil receives far less "inspiration" than before. The old "no-system" plan was, he felt, far more conducive "to developing individuality of character." In the process of becoming slaves to the routine of formal requirements, teachers lost their perspective and acquired "a tendency . . . to exaggerate little things—to sink the important." One effect of bureaucracy on behavior was to turn means into ends. All of the pressures on the teachers reinforced that effect. The city schoolman, by an "acquired bias of mind," had become a "martinet" who liked "the machine better the stiffer and firmer it can be made." By stressing the meek acceptance of orders from superiors, the system "narrows responsibility and stifles thought"; it thus becomes "death to all inventive minds."

The more perceptive critics, like Hinsdale and Charles Francis Adams, Jr., saw the dilemma that faced would-be educational reformers. Hinsdale was too shrewd and realistic to believe that anyone could reverse the direction of development and return to the old no-system plan of public education, even if it had in its day produced better results. Organization was necessary. Still, organization stamped out spontaneity and originality. Here was the dilemma, and to his credit Hinsdale recognized it in all its complexity. "You cannot have the greatest personal intrepidity and the best organization—the most individuality of character and the best organization—the most individuality of character and the most imposing array of school children and schoolmasters." "How," he asked, looking for a compromise, "shall we combine both elements most wisely?"

For all his perceptiveness, Hinsdale had little to offer in reply to his question; his only concrete suggestion was to prune and steamline the curriculum, which had become burdened with so many subjects that teachers, just to cover the ground, were forced into mechanical presentations. But that solution touched only the packed curriculum, which made rigid, crowded timetables a necessity; it did not provide ways of lessening the effects of a centralized, hierarchical structure on the teachers and pupils. In short, it missed the underlying dimensions of the problem and offered only a partial solution to the tough and troubling question Hinsdale had asked. No

one else, unfortunately, had a viable alternative to bureaucracy.

On the surface, the most promising alternative was offered
by Charles Francis Adams, Jr., but this, too, had serious deficiencies. More than any other critic, Adams accepted the need
for a planned hierarchical educational structure. His goal was
to reduce the mechanical, formalistic tone of the structure by
infusing it with new vigor and life. To accomplish this he proposed a revitalized superintending class trained "scientifically"
in universities.

The weakness of that prescription was that Adams was gen-
eralizing from his experience with a seemingly successful educational reform movement in Quincy, a town of only 10,000
people. He assumed that one intelligent man of magnetic personality, trained in educational science, could single-handedly
rejuvenate an entire bureaucratic school system, as Francis
Parker had done in Quincy, refining the necessary formal elements of that organization and simultaneously removing the
deadening effect of systematizing upon its spirit. Adams perceived the influence that the structure of an organization
could exert upon the temper of its operations and the personality of its participants, but he did not consider these effects
inevitable and predicted that a single inspired leader could
remove them. In a town of 10,000, charismatic bureaucracy
might work for a time, as Francis Parker had proved. But in a
city of hundreds of thousands, charismatic bureaucracy was a
very insubstantial model on which to place one's hopes for a
school system. Highly structured, hierarchical organizations
are far harder to change than Adams thought, as was demonstrated in Boston by the experience of both Adams's brother
Brooks (who obviously had been impressed with this model)
and, later on, by Francis Parker.

In Boston the reformers, who agreed with the analyses of
the critics of educational bureaucracy, assumed that they could

draw up a new blueprint for the city's schools and simply put it into effect. They realized that some resistance would come from teachers, especially grammar school masters, but they reasoned, incorrectly, that they could easily break the masters' hold on the system by installing the supervisors, who they hoped would prove to be charismatic bureaucrats, in the place of the masters. Through executive fiat, they expected, the conduct of an entire school system and all the relations within it could be successfully altered.

On January 28, 1879, the new school board revealed its reformist aspirations when it appointed a committee on the revision of the school system. Between January and May, the committee, pursuing the twin objectives of economizing and improving, scrutinized virtually every facet of the school system and, in a series of six reports, offered recommendations for sweeping changes. The leading spirit of the revision committee and the author of its reports was generally acknowledged to be Brooks Adams.

Some of the revision committee's many recommendations were designed, despite superfluous rationalizations, merely to save money. Among them were the proposals to abolish the kindergarten and the intermediate schools and to reorganize and centralize the high school system, the new scheme for furnishing supplies to students, and the elimination of special instructors. Others were intended to have a more direct educational effect. They included the pruning of the curriculum (as recommended by Hinsdale), the adoption of the newly designed grammar school course, and the upgrading of the normal school by raising admission standards, adding a postgraduate year, and increasing the amount of practice teaching. By the end of the year, one goal seemed clearly in sight; the board reported with pleasure that it had already reduced per-pupil spending in Boston, the highest in the nation, and expected the decrease to continue.

The most controversial and consequential recommendation

of the revision committee called for ending the supervision of the primary schools by the grammar school masters. Although this plan had once been necessary, it had never been entirely satisfactory in practice, argued the committee, because it made the masters both supervisors and teachers. To perform one duty well, they had to neglect the other; improvement in the primary schools was obtained at the expense of the grammar schools. Moreover, the masters diluted their influence by spreading it over a number of schools. For educational success, the committee was saying, personal appeal was as important as system, and it was this that the principalship of the masters had sacrificed.

As the committee analyzed the grammar school masters themselves, its real concerns began to emerge. Like lay reformers throughout the country, the committee believed that rigidity and formalism had stultified urban education, and reform required the exchange of mechanistic models and procedures for ones infused with vitality and enthusiasm. The results of the masters' principalship had been improvement, but it had been purchased with a needless circumscription of the "independence and individuality . . . of the subordinate instructors."

The reason lay in the effects of a hierarchical structure on personality, something the reformers in Boston realized quite as clearly as their counterparts around the country. Here the committee bared the part of its critique most galling to the masters and most certain to alienate those influential members of their school system. "The school-master," they wrote, "is proverbially dogmatic in his own sphere. . . . One tendency of his calling is to make him arbitrary." The supervision of the principals had been "overdone; and a check upon the tendency to 'machine school-keeping' [was required] not in the Primary Schools only, but also in the Grammar Schools."

To see how well the proposed new system would work, the

school board at the end of March placed one primary school under the care of a supervisor. Pleased with the results, the board decided to extend the experiment to all primary schools and consequently designated three supervisors to take charge of those schools. Superintendent Samuel Eliot showed his colors when he welcomed the change in primary school supervision and predicted its success in typically florid style. The school board and its new superintendent considered that education in Boston had become dry, rigid, and mechanistic, and the people who had permitted it to calcify were Philbrick, the man who had been superintendent for twenty-two years, and his loyal supporters, the grammar school masters. Reform required not only new curricula and more charismatic personnel but also a massive redistribution of power and influence. To effect such redistribution was the purpose of the removal of the grammar masters from the primary schools; to resist and sabotage this redistribution became the goal of the grammar school masters and their supporters.

Caught up in its desire to free the primary schools, the revision committee had neglected to consider the real unity and strength of the grammar school masters, whose close association and mutuality of interests had welded them into an influential informal organization (represented by the Boston Masters' Association) within the larger school system. For years, the masters had been meeting monthly for dinner and discussion of educational problems. Thus held together, the masters were in an effective position to undermine any educational reform they felt was unwise or threatening. By granting primary principalships, Philbrick had vastly increased the authority and power of the grammar school masters, making each of them, in a way, "a little king" in his district, and had thereby revealed his own shrewd sense of the conditions that create loyalty within a large organization.

Between Philbrick and the masters mutual loyalty and respect had developed, which reinforced the cohesiveness of the career schoolmen in the Boston system. Loyal to Philbrick, the masters had been enraged by his firing and were in no mood to cooperate with the board that had ousted him. In turn, when the masters were robbed of their power, Philbrick came to their defense with vigor. The sense of unity, the tight informal organization within the Boston school system, was something the reformers had been unable to perceive. Or, if they had perceived it, they were unable to realize that it was impossible to ride roughshod over such a group. They failed to understand that to introduce reforms they would have to have the masters on their side. Instead, the reformers (like their counterparts today) fomented a major battle, and in the end they lost.

The Defense of Bureaucracy: The Masters Counterattack

Opposition to the alteration in primary supervision arose quickly. After the publication of the first of the revision committee's reports in April, the *New England Journal of Education* violently attacked the proposed change. Afraid to speak out because of possible reprisals at the annual election, the masters published almost no criticism of the new arrangements, but their cause was championed by others, including the *Journal*, the prominent retired long-time Boston grammar master Joshua Bates, and, soon, Philbrick himself.

Philbrick, now newly distinguished, had returned from Paris early in 1880. Free of responsibility and the need to win re-election, he used his considerable influence to cause trouble for the school board and the supervisors. Philbrick bitterly resented the work of the revision committee, which destroyed many of the administrative features he had labored to introduce into the Boston school system. To Philbrick the committee's action represented a repudiation of his twenty-two years as superintendent, and he had no intention of receiving this insult in silence. He attended teachers' meetings, wrote letters to newspapers, meddled in the elections for the school board, and, most noticeably, between February and May, 1880, published a series of scathing articles in the *Journal of Education* reviewing the "new departure" in Boston. In these polemical articles Philbrick took apart, piece by piece, each of the changes instigated by the revision committee and, with much vehemence, the removal of the masters from the principalships of the primary schools.

Within the school board the masters had a few supporters, especially the retired master George Hyde. These men tried unsuccessfully to persuade the board to reverse its earlier decision and return the primary schools to the masters. At a school board meeting Hyde predicted (prophetically, as it turned out) "that within two years the primary schools would be under the charge of the masters, as they should be." The implication of impending counterattack in Hyde's remarks reflected an unofficial mobilization of professional forces in Boston and other cities as well.

Recall that schoolmen throughout the country were, like the Boston masters, under attack, and for many of the same reasons. The key men in the new urban school systems had to defend themselves against charges that they were contributing to a decline in the quality of public education by their rigid formalism, their exaltation of means over ends, their suppression of individuality, and their adoption of the personality and behavior of the drillmaster, revelling in the uniform, the petty, and the routine. To counter those serious accusations, educators in Boston and elsewhere developed a number of strategies. The opposition of the Boston grammar school masters and their supporters to the revision committee was one aspect of a larger counterattack against lay reformers across the country.

Representative of the attitude of schoolmen was the response of Cleveland's superintendent, ex-NEA president Andrew Rickoff, to Hinsdale's assertion that the quality of education had declined because of the development of highly differentiated, hierarchical, and uniform school systems. Rickoff's central argument was an open and unabashed defense of the type of educational system that had emerged in the cities. He insisted that graded schools, instead of hindering, helped the brightest pupils as well as the dullest by increasing the opportunities for individual attention. He extolled the reorganization of school systems on the principle of the division of labor, and he championed a centrally defined, rigid curriculum. By introducing plan and direction into education, a centrally planned syllabus spared the child from being buffeted back and forth between teachers with different ideas and approaches. "How," asked Rickoff, "shall unity of design in the fabric of education be guaranteed? We reply, in only one way, and that is by laying out our plans and specifications before the structure is commenced."

Rickoff's defense of a hierarchically structured, tightly organized, rigidly operated, centrally planned and directed school system made good sense in terms of efficiency. But, enmeshed in his school system as he had been for years, Rickoff was unable even to see what Hinsdale and other critics at their most perceptive had been deploring. Rickoff was unable, that is, to grasp the fact that Hinsdale and others had been lamenting the subtle effect of rigid structure on the temper of an institution and the personalities of its members. Because they were victims of this very effect, Rickoff and schoolmen who shared his views were simply unaware that there was any tension between originality and spontaneity, on the one hand, and efficiency in organization, on the other. For them there was no cost involved in building the increasingly characteristic administrative structure of urban education; bureaucratization was pure gain. It was, ironically, the inability of the schoolmen to appreciate the central point of the attacks that turned their defenses into sources of support for the accusations of their critics.

To defend bureaucracy on grounds of efficiency, harmony,

and rationality while ignoring its effects on the temper of the schools was a common strategy employed against critics of urban education. Another was to trim goals by bringing the objectives of public education into line with its actual achievements. Nowhere was this more evident than in the response of schoolmen to the accusations of Richard Grant White, the critic who aroused the most outrage and the most numerous counterattacks by arguing that the key assumption on which the case for public education had been advanced during the mid-century reform movement had been thoroughly disproved. The assumption, claimed White, was that public education was necessary to the social and moral life of a community: Education would bring about a decrease in crime, immorality, and other social ills. In part, White noted, the argument rested on a confusion of correlation with causation, because it assumed, from the frequent coexistence of ignorance and vice, that the former caused the latter. In reality, however, the two coexisted because they were both products of the same underlying problem: poverty. If the theory was true, White argued, then the tremendous investment in public education over several decades surely should have produced both a noticeable and measurable improvement in the quality of moral life and a decrease in crime. But everyone knew that the quality of life was steadily declining, that politics was ever more corrupt, that crime and vagrancy were on the increase. Despite massive attention to and expenditure on public education, asked White, "who needs to be told that in all these respects we have deteriorated?"

White damaged his clever case by using faulty statistics from the 1860 census, which, on the surface, seemed to show that Massachusetts, with a long tradition of public schools, had more crime, insanity, and suicide than Virginia, which, like most of the South, lagged in educational matters. But he was careful to insist that his argument not be taken to imply that education had caused the rise in crime and the decrease in morals. Rather, he emphasized, his point was simply that it had done nothing to stem these social maladies.

White's was one of the most damning and provocative indictments of public education America has seen, not so much for its denunciation of the lack of learning in the schools but for the way in which it hurled back the key assumptions of the school promoters. Although schoolmen had been arguing for decades that public schools would reform and uplift society both morally and economically, they too complained of the very social deficiencies that White lamented. If they admitted that society was still in a very bad way, then they were almost forced to accept the logic of White's ruthless argument, for public schools had been supported, maintained, and improved for a considerable period. Thus it followed clearly, in terms of the key arguments of the original mid-century promoters, that public schools had failed. The corollary was that the professional educators and planners of large, expensive school systems had likewise failed and were drawing their often sizable salaries on a fraudulent premise.

White's many attackers repeated the same points over and over again. One criticism was that his standing as an amateur made him incapable of judging the quality of education; another was that his attack revealed the antidemocratic animus that underlay most attacks on the schools; a third, and perhaps the most justified criticism was that his sources were faulty. But in all the rebuttals, White's professional critics refused to deal with his essential point that there was no essential relation between ignorance and crime, because both were products of poverty. In fact, most of them, including Philbrick, totally distorted the point in their attempts to discredit White, claiming, incorrectly, that White had asserted education caused crime.

Schoolmen explicitly and vigorously denied the accuracy of White's interpretation of the purpose of public education, although they did not generally state their version of the true theory. One reason they felt no need to offer proof that White was wrong was that in 1873 a group of prominent educators (including Philbrick), under the leadership of William Torrey Harris, had published a credo, widely taken as the official statement of the theory of education in the United States, and they considered reference to that statement sufficient to refute White's contentions about the social role of public schools both past and present. Any reading of earlier theorists like Horace Mann would show, they maintained, that public schools had never been viewed as social panaceas. Here White's critics were wrong, as Chapter 1 should have made clear. In contrast to Mann, the *Statement of Theory of Education* had a very different tone. It contained no passionate metaphors and no predictions that the school would conquer social ills; in sober, unemotional language, thoroughly unlike Mann's, it merely stated that *one* function of the school in America was "to train the pupil into habits of prompt obedience to his teachers and the practice of self-control in its various forms, in order that he may be prepared for a life wherein there is little police-restraint on the part of the constituted authorities." Although the tone of the later statement was less emotional, the idea that schools existed to promote law and order remained central to educational thought.

The sober and modest 1873 document, devoid of boastful or extravagant claims, is typical of the period. Parallels to Mann's emotional and optimistic rhetoric, quite common among those concerned with educational innovation and administration in the 1840's and 1850's, would be hard indeed to find in the 1870's and 1880's. The disagreement between White and his professional critics about the role of education is particularly significant because of the process it reveals. In the 1840's education promoters had labored to convert the people to the cause of public schools, which they evangelically described as prerequisites to a secular millennium. Their successors, the second generation of public school leaders, inherited the school systems that had been established by the mid-century innovators. As the new systems manifestly did not reach their original goals, the stated aims of education were gradually and quietly displaced by more limited and realistic expectations. This displacement was necessary because school administrators could no longer rely on the predictions of Horace Mann to justify the massive and expensive organizations they operated and expanded. The very survival of public education as a series of large bureaucratic school systems depended on the transformation of expectations. It was a real question, though, whether the survival of their organizations had become more important to schoolmen than the quality of education and the real needs of children.

Proclaiming the virtues of bureaucratic organizations, pointing out the enormous difficulties posed for the schools by their context, toning down the expectations for public education—these were the rhetorical strategies of defense used by career educators. In Boston and elsewhere definite activities were added, most notably the development of professional journals and organizations on a new scale. By the 1870's there existed a body of educators large enough and permanently and seriously enough concerned with schools to support national periodicals and to make regional and national organizations more viable.

The publications and organizations fostered, for one thing, a sense of community among administrators and teachers. In the pages of journals and at meetings, they had the satisfaction of sharing their problems and anxieties and knowing that they were by no means alone in their difficulties. The publications also gave them a forum in which to express criticism with relative safety. For instance, in its articles and editorial columns, the *New England Journal of Education* (as of 1881, when it became national, just *Journal of Education*) offered a strong and articulate defense of the career educators against lay critics, as well as a national platform from which to launch a counterattack. The editor, Thomas Bicknell, was in an ideal position to provide the schoolmen with support, for it was on *their* support, not on that of school boards or any other segment of the lay public, that the success of his journal depended. Bicknell thus could say what many others, circumscribed by insecure political situations, could only feel. It was through Bicknell, to take only one instance, that the Boston grammar school masters were able to mount their strong and ultimately successful counteroffensive against their critics. The potential that schoolmen saw in professional organization is illustrated clearly by the establishment in 1881 of the National Council of Education as a part of the NEA. Most fittingly, its first president was Bicknell. The council considered itself a forum for mediating the claims of the many new and conflicting ideas for educational innovation. Although it had no power of compulsion, the council hoped that stamping a particular point of view with its imprimatur would substantially influence educational practice, a critical consideration at that moment because of the combination of widespread acerbic criticism leveled at public education and serious disagreement on some important issues among educators themselves.

The experience of the Boston grammar school masters reinforced Bicknell's contentions, for their internal unity and lack of contention were precisely their source of strength. In Boston, opposition to reform took the form not only of protests by supporters of the masters but also of covert and hard-to-prove resistance by the masters themselves. As one commentator noted, the masters did not like the new arrangement and, "therefore, have tried . . . to ridicule the new system and throw obstacles in its way." It was widely believed, and probably with justification, that the masters were doing all they could to subvert the new supervisory arrangements. Without writing in the journals or otherwise opening themselves to demonstrable charges of insubordination, the masters used their strategic position, their combination of prestige, influence, and informal organization, their cohesiveness, to plan and execute tactics that would harass and destroy the "new departure."

The Triumph of Informal Organization: The Victory of the Masters

The hostility of the masters and the controversy within the system were too much for Samuel Eliot. The superintendent was unable—indeed, did not even try—to do anything to reduce the hostility between the reformist board and the masters. In fact, he had exacerbated the situation by taking the reformist side and alienating the masters. Unable to contain, much less resolve, the controversy, Eliot resigned in the middle of 1880, ostensibly because of ill health.

Apparently the attitude of the grammar school masters influenced the choice of the new superintendent, the principal of Boston English High School, Edwin Seaver, for he was a candidate welcomed by them and by the *New England Journal of Education*. Like Philbrick, Seaver quickly showed that he understood the need for the support of his teachers. At the first monthly meeting of the masters after his election, Seaver outlined "the motives which would govern his action." The editor of the *Journal* remarked slyly, "It was very fitting, too, that he should thank the teachers for the sympathy extended to him as well as for the congratulations." Seaver suggested to the masters that, when a policy they had criticized was adopted by the school board, "it would be the part of wisdom to 'let it run its race and be glorified,' or condemned." After the meeting Seaver "took his usual place at the monthly dinner of the masters, and that body . . . seemed indeed to justify the remark of one of the most eminent of their number, that they were 'very, very, happy again.'" With the appointment of Seaver and the consequent reunion of superintendent and masters, the strength in the controversy shifted markedly to the schoolmen. The denouement became simply a matter of time. But before the final actions had been taken, Boston passed through some more trials that revealed the inability of its bureaucracy to accommodate charismatic and individualistic personalities, for Francis Parker came to Boston, bringing with him one-fourth of Quincy's erstwhile teachers. It was not surprising that school reformers in Boston were eager to lure Parker to their city, and in 1881 the combination of a salary double the one he received in Quincy and the parsimoniousness of the Quincy school board, which made it unable to retain its best teachers, prompted Parker to accept the offer of a supervisorship in the Hub. "It is said," reported a very knowledgeable observer, that when Parker left Quincy he received this advice from Charles Francis Adams: "Get a new suit of clothes, a tall hat, and keep your mouth shut, if you wish to succeed." The advice was excellent, but Parker refused to heed at least the last part, and that contributed quite directly to his failure to work the revolution in Boston that he had in Quincy.

The appointment of Parker as a supervisor with special responsibility for Boston's primary schools revealed one goal of the reformist faction: the introduction of the Quincy system into the Boston primary schools. Most likely this objective had contributed to the school board's decision to remove the masters from the primary schools, for the masters were skeptical of the sort of innovation Parker represented. Stern traditionalists, they looked with skepticism on most of Parker's methods, especially the use of oral instruction, the relaxation of discipline, and the attempt to introduce "sunshine in the schoolroom."

Parker apparently decided that he would run his section of the city as he had run the schools of Quincy—personally and as he saw fit, with little reference to established procedures or even to the school board itself. He determined, so the story went, to prove the superiority of his system to all others by introducing it into the Prince School in Back Bay, where the rivalry from excellent prestigious private schools was keenest. Success gained in this school "would be relatively of greater importance than successes scored in two or three of our public schools elsewhere." To create his demonstration, Parker wanted to put a particular teacher from Quincy into the Prince School; his problem was that no vacancies existed there. So he decided to make one and executed a complex maneuver, described by his subsequent accusers as a game of checkers. The victim of Parker's game was Lydia A. Isbell, fourth assistant in the Blossom Street School. Mrs. Isbell, a widow who had grown up in the district of Boston in which she later taught, had served in the Blossom Street School for seventeen consecutive years. Her total service, in fact, had been nearly thirty years. After marriage she had moved West with her husband and had returned when he died. A popular and morally faultless lady who had taught many of the children and adults of the district, she had received a rating of "second," or "good," from previous supervisors. Parker rated her sixth, or "bad, very bad." His district committee, allegedly now completely under his sway, agreed to fire Mrs. Isbell summarily. Then the series of moves Parker had planned became clear. Miss Freeman of the Poplar Street School was to take Mrs. Isbell's place; the place of Miss Freeman was to be filled by Miss Kendrick of the Prince School, and into the now vacant position in the demonstration school was to go Parker's favorite from Quincy. An additional complication was Parker's admission that his Quincy teacher "could not compete with girls from the high and normal schools" in the standard teacher's examination, a problem he overcame by bullying the committee to waive the test.

The firing of Mrs. Isbell was too much for both the opponents of Parker and the residents of the Blossom Street district. They tried unsuccessfully to persuade the school committee to reinstate Mrs. Isbell. A number of "the most worthy citizens of West Boston protested, and a petition, signed by

Reverend C. A. Bartol, Alderman Slade, Thomas Gaffield [a retired merchant], F. T. Connell and others was sent to the School Board for a hearing." Under pressure from many people, the board had little choice, and as its hearing into the dismissal of Mrs. Isbell proceeded the full facts of the case emerged for the first time.

The hearing itself turned into a violent attack on Parker, led by Gaffield, and resulted in a thorough public condemnation of Parker. He had gone too far. Amid the bureaucratic uniformity of the Boston school system his individualistic style, his contempt for regulations and standard operating procedures, emerged in a harsh and glaring light. After the facts became public at the hearing, the school board had little choice, and only Brooks Adams supported Parker. The board officially reinstated Mrs. Isbell in her school; Parker had been beaten.

It is not surprising that Parker soon left Boston. Parker was a man who simply could not tolerate the climate of an urban school system, and the system really could not tolerate him. Parker had to be able to control and transform any organization of which he was a member. Talented, egotistic, and ambitious, he could not brook opposition, delay, or the frustrations of trying to reform urban schools. He was the sort of man who works well in a small town or city like Quincy or, even better, in a normal school, where his influence could extend to every member. Parker's experience in Boston revealed the incompatibility of charisma and bureaucracy; it showed up the utopianism of those who proclaimed that a single enlightened and magnetic man could transform a large urban school system; and it provided evidence that even Charles Francis Adams, Jr., the most realistic critic of the time, had not given urban schools an alternative to rigid and formalistic bureaucracy. Essentially it was on charismatic bureaucracy that the Boston reformers had placed their hopes: Able outsiders hired as supervisors were to break the grip of the masters and, by their personal influence, reform the temper of the schools. One reason the reformers failed was their reliance on this implausible scheme.

By the end of 1881 it was clear that the direction of events within the Boston school system was still changing in favor of the masters and their supporters. For one thing, prosperity had returned, and the need for economizing was no longer urgent. At the city Democratic convention in 1881, only the chairman's vote renominated Brooks Adams for the school board; with this evidence of dissatisfaction, he withdrew. The withdrawal of Adams and the election of Gaffield, the retired merchant who was Mrs. Isbell's knight, symbolized the shift of educational opinion, reflected, too, in the letters to newspapers calling for a return to the old system. Some of the letters came from Philbrick, who, sensing that the city was ripe for change, vitriolically denounced the school board members and called on the voters to turn them out of office *en masse*.

Although only four of its twelve recently elected members were new, the school board of 1882 gave indications from the beginning of the year that change was imminent. Predictably, in early February members of the school board offered two motions, one to return the principalship of the primary schools to the grammar school masters, and the other to subordinate the supervisors to the superintendent by making them assistant superintendents.

The supporters of the schoolmen were not slow to point out the significance of the vote at which the former recommendation, with only slight modification, was passed. One called it clear proof that John Dudley Philbrick had been right all the time. The editor of the *Journal of Education* termed the restoration a vindication of the "old regime" and proclaimed that the teachers of the city found it a "famous victory." Despite their weak, untenured position, the masters had shown their real strength; the struggle and their eventual victory demonstrated that the day had passed when a school

committee could impose reform without the support of its
teaching staff. Alienated by the reform movement, the masters,
with the support of the *Journal of Education,* had effectively
prevented the successful operation of the "new departure."
An influential and cohesive unofficial group within the larger
school system, the masters had proved that without their approval no school policy could succeed. The reformers, blind to
the constraints that impede changes within complex organizations, had failed to realize the potency of the masters and had
blithely proceeded to innovate with full confidence that, as
the legal masters of the system, they could work changes at
will. They learned otherwise, as has each succeeding generation
of reformers ever since.

Although no substantive changes were introduced during
the next year, 1883, restoration of harmony continued, and
the good feelings proved not to be transient. Comments from
even formerly hostile sources underlined the transformed atmosphere described by the board. Really, all that remained
for the counterrevolution was to make the superintendent in
law—according to the regulations, that is—the true head of
the school system. When this happened at last in 1884, the
Boston bureaucracy was truly complete. The centralization
and addition of supervisory personnel effected by the 1876 reorganization had run counter to the principles underlying bureaucracies in some critical ways. They had left the definition
of roles unclear and assigned the same administrative duties
to different individuals. Instead of a smoothly efficient hierarchy, the changes had introduced confusion and controversy
into the school system. Reformers, moreover, had violated
bureaucratic canons by appointing laymen to high office instead of promoting them from the ranks. Now, at least, these
problems had been solved. The supervisors had been given a
definite place in the hierarchy; functions had been differentiated more clearly; control had been centralized more firmly;
some Boston masters had even been elected supervisors. The

anomalies that made bureaucracy only incipient in the plans of Henry Barnard or in towns like Quincy had been removed. In fact as well as on paper, the Boston school system had become a proper bureaucracy. Other American cities soon followed its example.

One consequence of bureaucratization, Amitai Etzioni has pointed out, is the separation of consumption, those who are served by an organization, from control, those who direct it. This distinction points up a significant aspect of the bureaucratization of American urban education: the altered relation of the school to the community. As the organization of urban education became more complex, schools were increasingly divorced from the communities they served, and laymen had progressively less power to influence school policy. In turn, schoolmen themselves gained augmented power to run the schools as they saw fit, with little or no reference to the actual requirements of the community. From one point of view, it certainly was desirable for career educators to acquire the autonomy necessary to free them from meddling and uninformed interference. But from another point of view, the ability to resist community opinion, revealed by the success of the Boston masters against the reformers, contributed to the sterility of urban education. Needing to communicate only with one another, with many legitimate concerns for their own status, power, and protection, schoolmen, whenever attacked, have been quick to withdraw into the protective shell of their massive school systems. Bureaucratization has lessened their sensitivity to their communities, to their students, and to the informed and constructive criticism that would make progress possible. The reaction of schoolmen to the voice of lay criticism became a defensive reflex as the traditions of resistance forming in the nineteenth century calcified into hardened and ingrained responses.

The conflicting needs for both autonomy and responsiveness in educational systems was one dilemma posed by the bureaucratization of education. Another was the problem of finding an alternative model of educational organization. For the most part, the alternatives that seemed alive in 1850 no longer appeared viable in 1875. During the later nineteenth century, perceptive critics were fully aware that public education required some form of rational organization. They clearly saw the tension between vitality and responsiveness, on the one hand, and the demands of a complex administrative task, on the other. Knowing that they could not dispense with formal structure, they still looked for alternatives to the rigidly hierarchical models that had emerged. But all proposed solutions were inadequate; no one had a viable alternative. The problem has not disappeared. Critics of the schools have continued to lament their rigid and formalistic features, their negative influence on the personality of teachers and students, their inability to accommodate highly individualistic styles of conduct. But an organizational alternative to overcome these deficiencies is still to be formulated; despite nearly a century of criticism, American education still lacks a real alternative model to hierarchical bureaucracy.

3

Twentieth-Century School Reform:
Notes Toward a History*

The structure of American urban education has not changed since late in the nineteenth century; by 1880, the basic features of public education in most major cities were the same as they are today. The absence of those characteristics in some places did not reflect a different pattern of educational development; it represented, rather, a slower rate of urban growth. In time these places too acquired the distinctive marks of American urban education.

Continuities in Educational Structure

Beyond doubt, there have been educational developments and innovations of first-rate importance since the late nineteenth century. Consider, for instance, the kindergarten, the junior high school, industrial education, testing, the new math. Each has brought about change; but—and this is the

---

* Parts of this chapter, in a slightly different form, appeared in a review of Gross and Gross, eds., *Radical School Reform* (copyright 1970 Saturday Review, Inc.) and are reprinted here by permission of the *Saturday Review*.

important point—it is change *within* a given structure that itself has not altered. That is the basis on which we can claim continuity in American education over almost a century.

What were the features fixed so firmly by the late nineteenth century? Most succinctly, public education was universal, tax-supported, free, compulsory, bureaucratically arranged, class-biased, and racist. That those characteristics existed by 1880 should be evident from the preceding chapters. Their continuity is not hard to demonstrate.

By 1880 most people went to school for at least some period of time. The enormous expansion of high school enrollment in the early twentieth century did not represent a break with tradition but, rather, the continuation and acceleration of a trend that had been in motion since at least the middle of the nineteenth century. Continuous increase in the average school-leaving age has been a pronounced feature of educational history, and waves of attendance have swept upward through the common school, through the high school, and now, nearly, through the college.

Continuities in finance appear even more clearly than in attendance patterns. Despite well-documented inadequacies, property taxation remains the principal source of educational revenue, and gross inequalities continue to mark different regions and even neighboring communities. The federal funding provided by the Elementary and Secondary Education Act of 1965 in principle represents a significant departure in school finance, but the sums it has provided thus far are pitifully small compared to the total cost of education.

Similarly, education has remained free. In fact, like school attendance, the scope of free education has expanded. The significant debate has moved, over the course of a century, from the propriety of providing free common schools to free high schools and, now, to free higher education. It is carried on within the framework of the assumption that the public should provide and pay for a complete system of formal schooling. There is controversy about the limits of that system, but the assumption, injected with such force into public consciousness by mid-nineteenth-century schoolmen, remains unchallenged.

Nor has the compulsory nature of schooling changed. By the late nineteenth century the public in most places had accepted the concept of compulsion, although the enforcement of compulsory laws remained uncertain and inefficient. Compulsion had followed with inexorable logic from the expectations people had for their schools and from the relationship they perceived between schooling and public welfare, as I hope the earlier discussion has made clear. Its diffusion is evidence, once more, of the similarity of educational purpose and organization throughout the country. Compulsion has become woven into the structure of education and into the popular mind; it is no longer a radical solution to a problem but part of the conventional wisdom, as the following incident illustrates. Only a few years ago the Massachusetts legislature passed a comprehensive new school law and, in the process, repealed all the old laws. The day after passage, to the dismay of the legislature, it was discovered that compulsory education had been repealed unwittingly. Immediately, the governor drafted a bill; it passed the legislature at once and without demur.

As we have seen, the Boston school system had become a bureaucracy, in every sense of that term, by 1875. By that date, other school systems had become bureaucratic as well, and those that had not followed their example by early in the twentieth century. It is not necessary to point out the extent to which bureaucracy remains the organizational form of urban education today. What is of particular interest about the contemporary situation is that bureaucracy itself has become an objective of reform assault, as it has not been for some time. But contemporary attempts to reduce the bureaucratic element in urban education appear to be no more successful than earlier ones were, and the problems that frustrated and finally defeated the Boston School Committee and Francis Parker in the late 1870's seem as prominent today as then.

Formulation of the relationships between bureaucracy and class bias remains a major task of social historians and social theorists. My earlier discussion of incipient bureaucratic models and of the mediating function of organizations represents only a beginning. Nevertheless, although we lack an adequate statement of relationships, we can be quite sure that some connection did exist. We have seen that bureaucratic forms developed early in the history of public schooling; we have observed as well that class bias was reflected in the educational aims of the same period. Bureaucracy was the form of organization best suited to the realization of those aims, and it is in this fact that the relationship between class and bureaucracy lies. Sociological and administrative theory generally assumes a functional—and, implicitly, inevitable—relationship between urban industrial society and bureaucratic organization. Given the complexity of society, it is believed, business cannot be arranged otherwise. However, it is not impossible to imagine different arrangements for social institutions, such as schools, as contemporary exponents of decentralization are proving. In fact, bureaucracy is inevitable only if social complexity is approached with certain particular values and priorities. If order, efficiency, and uniformity are preferred to responsiveness, variety, and flexibility, then, indeed, bureaucracy is inevitable.

But order, efficiency, and uniformity, values that have permeated public education since the nineteenth century, have strong class overtones. That has been shown in a variety of ways in the preceding chapters. Perhaps the strongest impulse behind the founding of public educational systems was what today we would call the urge for law and order, or the attempt to socialize the urban poor to behavior that will decrease crime, diminish expenditures on public welfare, promote safety on the streets, and contribute to industrial productivity. Early school promoters convinced their constituencies that public education would accomplish those ends, and their imminent attainment has been confidently predicted ever since. Despite overwhelming disconfirming evidence, faith in the power—the essentially conservative power—of schooling has persisted, and this is one of the great puzzles in the history of American thought.

One reason relates to the problem of finding nonsocialist approaches to social reform. An official ideology that emphasizes the importance of free enterprise and shuns state intervention has limited alternatives with which to approach major social problems, such as poverty. Massive income redistribution or broad-scale intervention in the economy generally has not been acceptable. Education, on the other hand, has appeared to be an immediate and effective solution to social problems. There is a surface logic, which remains immensely appealing: Equipping children with appropriate skills and attitudes can cause the problems of unemployment and poverty to disappear. The illnesses of society become diagnosed as simply a lack of education, and the prescription for reform becomes more education. The prescription, for one thing, unleashes a flurry of seemingly purposeful activity and, for another, requires no tampering with basic social structural or economic characteristics, only with the attitudes of poor people, and that has caused hardly a quiver. The problem (and the determination with which people have refused to admit it is powerful testimony to the usefulness of the idea) is that this approach to social reform simply has not worked. In fact, insofar as it has been a smoke screen, obscuring the nature of social problems, educational reform has hindered broader social reform.

The other reason that the power of schooling has remained an article of faith rests on the class bias inherent in the actual structure and functioning of school systems. Educational rhetoric to the contrary notwithstanding, it is the children of the well-to-do, not the children of the poor, who have benefited most from public education. That is especially true of the higher levels of schooling, one important function of which has been to secure differential advantage to the children of the affluent. Throughout the history of education there have been essentially two levels of schooling: one virtually universal, and the other attended by a minority of the eligible children. There is, as I said earlier, little evidence to point out where that minority came from, but what there is indicates that it was largely the children of the affluent. When the common school had become universal, for instance, the children who attended high school represented the more prosperous sections of the community. Today, when high school is virtually universal, the same is true of the students at public universities.

This means that the continuous extension of educational facilities has been, and continues to be, primarily in the interests of the affluent in a very direct and immediate sense. That extension first of all spreads to the community as a whole the financial burden of providing a minority, and a select minority, of the children with an economic advantage over the rest. At the same time, it operates as a continuous social sorting device enabling well-to-do children to retain or improve their advantage while doing very little for the rest. The notion that schooling secures differential advantages to the poor covers this situation very nicely.

Public education represents a social sorting device stacked even more heavily against blacks than against the poor. Racism remains as integral and functional to public education as ever. An attitude that describes one group of people as essentially different from, and inferior to, the dominant group is racist. From this perspective, as I have argued earlier, racism underlay the origins of public education; for the poor, especially the Irish Catholic poor, appeared to school promoters in exactly those terms. The racism implicit in the origins of public education became functional as an excuse for educational failure. Newly created systems of public education failed to meet the ends for which they had been established, and some explanation became necessary. The same problem faced the managers of newly created reform schools, prisons, and mental hospitals. In each case, including that of public education, they created a defense in terms of the inferiority of their inmates. That inferiority, it was argued, was hereditary; thus, given the inferior stock with which they had to contend, what could one expect?

Thought about education, crime, mental illness, and delinquency has oscillated between stresses on environment and on heredity. Both have had racist implications, the latter more blatantly. Generally speaking, environmentalism has been optimistic and hence characteristic of movements of reform. Thus it dominated reform thought in the 1840's and surfaced again at the end of the century and in the early 1960's. In each case, the reappearance of an emphasis on heredity has accompanied the frustration of reformist expectations and the waning of reformist zeal. That happened in the 1860's and again in the early twentieth century; it happened again in 1969, when Arthur R. Jensen, a leading educational psychologist, published an influential article ascribing lower native intelligence to blacks than to whites. The article followed and built upon the vaguely pessimistic conclusions of the Coleman report on *Equality of Educational Opportunity* that the quality of schooling does not matter and of the Commission on Civil Rights on *Racial Isolation in the Public Schools* that compensatory education has failed. Jensen's thesis has been eagerly seized upon by a variety of strange bedfellows, from Southern white supremacists to big-city school people anxious to excuse their own ineptitude.

The racism sometimes inherent in the environmentalist position (where environment is defined as the *family* context) is more subtle, and for that reason often more insidious. Its genteel wrapping covers its animus; the general tone is pity for the deprived slum child, who lacks opportunities to learn manners and morals, to see cows and trees, to learn long words and respect for education. The bias in this attitude is apparent on a moment's reflection, as the following example should make clear: It is considered an instance of cultural deprivation if a slum child cannot identify a cow but not if a suburban child is unable to identify a cockroach. This attitude strenuously avoids condemning the child and places the blame on his background. It views the job of the school as massively compensatory. In one form or another, the argument has been put forward since the nineteenth century. Its sponsors consistently have failed to see that it is condescending and patronizing, or offensive, to the poor themselves. Two ways in which it is particularly insidious should be observed; first of all, it teaches the child to regard his parents and his home with an emotion ranging between pity and contempt. Second, it removes responsibility for educational failure from the teacher and school fully as much as the hereditary position. Translated into practical terms, the environmental position also permits the school to excuse itself, or to lessen its effort, in view of the homes from which the students come. Given all those obstacles of environment, the well-meaning liberal teacher might well ask, what can I be expected to do?

Today, obviously, the notion of cultural deprivation expresses the environmentalist point of view. Although its proponents sometimes assume that their concept is novel, in fact it stretches back well into the nineteenth century. The image of the poor in educational thought has shifted from the depraved to the deprived during the last century; the basis of the argument has moved from moralism to social psychology. But the direction, the animus, and—need it be stressed?—the racism remain.

Urban public school systems present a curious amalgam of inherent structural and ideological defects; it is no wonder that they have failed. They have not reformed society; they have not won the allegiance of the poor and the black; they have not bound Americans to each other in affection and respect. They have been erected first and foremost upon a soft, evasive intellectual base; they have depended on a continued reluctance to compare their actual and official functions or their stated and operative purposes. They have developed organizational structures that moved them ever farther away from interaction with the communities they served, and, finally, they have even refused to accept responsibility for educating anybody successfully in anything. Once granted a captive audience, they have had little need to succeed; it has been easier to develop a battery of excuses that place the blame for educational failure outside the school and on the home.

This situation immediately raises another historical problem: Why have reform movements failed to change these characteristics of urban education? In particular, what of progressive education? The answer to that question is implicit in what I have written already. It is sad but true that an understanding of earlier reform efforts and their failures permits us to make general predictions about others. Of the reform thrust known as progressivism in the late nineteenth and early twentieth centuries I have said little, quite deliberately. My contention is that the shape of public education in American cities had been fixed before progressivism began. Progressivism failed to alter that shape. It failed partly because it suffered from the weaknesses of earlier reform movements. It failed as well because it did not even try. For the most part, progressivism represented a conservative movement that accepted the structure of American education as it was and tried to work changes within that framework.

Progressivism and Education

The term "progressive education" immediately conjures up a host of images: John Dewey, the child-centered school, the project method, Auntie Mame. But to accept those images uncritically would be a drastic oversimplification. Progressive is an umbrella label, and not a very satisfactory one at that, for a wide variety of activities directed toward changing American political and institutional behavior between, roughly, 1890 and World War I. The relations between reform efforts in education and in other places are intimate, complex, and hardly disentangled yet by historians. In education alone, progressivism refers to activities on a variety of planes; sometimes they overlapped, sometimes they remained quite separate. But any comprehensive analysis of progressivism must include them all. Most succinctly, they are (1) the attempt to alter the political control of education, (2) the reformulation of educational thought, (3) the introduction of educational innovations, (4) the promotion of pedagogical change, and (5) the injection of scientific management into administrative practice.

At this juncture, discussion of these activities and their interrelationships must be more or less speculative. Historians have done astoundingly little research on any of them, with the possible exception of educational thought, and even there they have largely confined themselves to leading theorists and neglected the attitudes of teachers, administrators, and various public groups. They have neglected, even more, the working out of reform efforts on the local level. Consequently, we have almost no case studies that trace attitudes and developments in particular communities and try to find out exactly what sorts of change happened in schools. Some, although woefully little, work on these topics has begun in the last few years, and the first results are just appearing. Thus, it is peculiarly difficult to write meaningfully about educational reform in the progressive period. What follows, therefore, is a series of hunches about how the history of that period will look when the evidence is in.

At one level, progressivism meant municipal reform; that was the case for both city politics and education. Throughout the country, coalitions of urban reformers tried to replace the bosses who governed American cities, to reform the legal structure of city government, and to increase the efficiency of municipal services. Their campaigns combined moral indignation at corruption with a protest at the high cost of graft and inefficiency, and in city after city they exposed major scandals. Education formed part of the municipal system that needed cleaning up. School systems provided patronage in the form of jobs, contracts, and supplies, and city political machines had not been backward about exploiting their potential. As part of their effort to improve municipal government, reformers sought to change the nature and source of educational control. For the most part, they proposed the centralization of power in a small school board with members elected at large. That would replace the large boards with members elected from wards, and it was ward politics that was particularly associated with political machines. A small central board representing the entire city, reformers felt, would be more independent of political influences. It would be the job of the new board to introduce the regulations and procedures that would replace nepotism and graft with equity, efficiency, and good business practices.

Two features of this reform are especially relevant to the analysis of progressivism in education. First, it reflected very little concern for children. Political and economic considerations dominated the movement; educational ones remained quite marginal. Second, it represented a class effort. The small amount of historical work that has been done on the composition of reform groups finds them largely controlled by old-stock first citizens, quite often professionals. Municipal reform represented as much a thrust for power by this group as it did a moral crusade for good government. Bossism, ward politics, and immigrants were linked together in public attitudes. Consequently, an anti-immigrant and anti-working-class attitude underlay much of municipal reform. It would be instructive to analyze overlapping membership in municipal-reform and immigrant-restriction associations; I suspect it would be substantial.

Educational reform reflected these biases. The men and women concerned with altering the control of education had no higher opinion of poor city families than did their predecessors a half-century before. They shared the anti-immigrant sentiments and the racism of their class. Insofar as their reform efforts had an educational purpose, that goal again reflected one of the larger aims of municipal reform: the attempt to find new modes of social control appropriate to a dynamic and fluid urban environment. Their aim remained similar to that of earlier reformers: inculcating the poor with acceptable social attitudes. This has had important implications. It has meant that the government of school systems has continued to rest on a disdain for a large portion of students and their families. This has only widened the gulf between working-class communities and schools that mid-century reformers had helped to create. Schools remained distant and alien institutions to the poor, the bureaucratic detachment of the staff reinforced by the bias of those in political control of the system.

It is the tradition of distance and disdain that has led to the confrontation between black communities and school systems in recent times. The hostile reaction of school boards like Boston's in the 1960's to the problem of *de facto* segregation, for instance, revealed how the long-standing insensitivity of a school system to its poorer clientele had hardened into a pattern of interacting with community groups. Incident after incident suggested that the school board simply did not care to try to understand the aspirations of some black people; it appeared, very simply, that the wishes of black people did not matter much. That open confrontation has now broken out in some areas should surprise no one. It is the legacy of school government cut off from and insensitive to the community it serves.

The relationship between municipal reform and the formulation of educational theory remains to be explored. As it is usually understood, progressive educational thought appears to be radically different in tone and intention from the movement for political control. Professor Lawrence Cremin, in *Transformation of the School*, has provided a sympathetic and incisive intellectual history of progressive thought that reinforces its traditional image. The difficulty with Cremin's version is its inability to relate theory to action, to connect politics with educational reform. For Cremin portrays educational theory as broadly humane and democratic—even, at times, libertarian. It lacks, in his account, the impulse to social control and social order apparent in progressive political activity. According to Cremin, educational progressivism was a branch of political progressivism, and he views the latter as moved by the same generous impulses as the educational theory he describes. The problem lies in his version of political progressivism, which historians are steadily replacing with one similar to the interpretation sketched above. Either educational theory and political reform developed along different lines, or the interpretation of that theory must undergo a revision comparable to the interpretation of other aspects of reform.

As we have come to view it, progressive educational thought stressed the incorporation of the experience of the child into the development of the curriculum, the softening of pedagogy, the breaking down of barriers between subjects, and the active participation of the learner. At its best, as in Dewey's formulation, educational theory combined a focus on the child and his world with a driving social-reformist commitment that, in the tradition of American educational thought, saw education as the key to social uplift.

The child-centered and the social reformist are two of the important strands in progressive educational thought. A third is the scientific. At times the three strands coexisted, as in the writings of Dewey; at other times strains between priorities drove them apart. The scientific assumed an independent existence most notably. Educational psychology, in particular, lost the broad social and philosophic concerns apparent in the writings of early theorists, especially Dewey, and narrowed its focus, concentrating on testing and the measurement of individual differences. The IQ test and the abuses of measurement remain heirs to the progressive tradition in education and, indeed, in American thought, fully as much as the contemporary movement for free schools. Progressive reformers of all varieties attempted to utilize the methods and findings of science in the promotion of their goals.

Dewey, it is true, resisted the increasing divorce of science and philosophy in educational theory as well as the other sectarian excesses of progressive educators. Nonetheless, there is a darker side to the social thought of even the best progressives, notably Dewey and Jane Addams, and it is that aspect of their writing that is congruent with the impulses at work in municipal reform. The point is complex, and it has just begun to be developed by historians, particularly Clarence Karier and Paul Violas. Briefly, the emphasis on community in Jane Addams and the definitions of democracy and experience in Dewey provide particularly subtle and sophisticated instances of the widespread attempt in their time to foster modes of social control appropriate to a complex urban environment. Most starkly, both Addams and Dewey in the last analysis stressed the subservience of individual will and aspiration to those of the group. Dewey's educational ideal, it has been pointed out often enough, did not leave the child unregulated and alone; it retained a strong guiding role for the teacher. That role became largely the creation of an environment, a carefully planned group context that would provide children with a sequence of experiences, which, despite their apparent spontaneity, were in fact meticulously elicited. Those experiences would lead the children to develop habitual ways of responding, to internalize the norms of democratic living. The key to democracy for Dewey was in action; democracy was not a static form but a mode of living, a way of behaving in which each person continually referred his actions and his desires to the well-being of the group. Education, by implication, served to instill conformist behavior, a set of inner controls that would make external social controls unnecessary. This for Jane Addams was the function of community. Both she and Dewey were acutely conscious of the decline of traditional social controls in urban and industrial settings; both saw a need to accommodate industrial workers to their work. They emphasized the importance of teaching assembly-line workers the importance of their task and its place in the larger processes of production. This was, as it is usually presented, an effort to relieve the tedium and mental drudgery of manual work. But its larger social function, the result if it worked, would be to socialize workers to contentment and to increase their identification with their industry.

Despite their subtle coercive implications, Dewey's educational proposals represented a vast improvement over most contemporary practice. Unfortunately, he did little to implement their adoption other than to establish a model school. In fact, his writings generally fail to deal with the relationship between the structure of school systems and the content of education. He did not ask, that is, whether it was possible to effect a reform of pedagogy within the bureaucratic structure of urban schools. That question was left largely unexplored by progressive theorists, which is one of the central weaknesses of their writings. For, if radical structural alteration must precede significant pedagogical change, then the first efforts of school reformers must be directed toward breaking down the bureaucratic form of schooling and changing the nature of its political control. That this is the case certainly forms part of the argument of educational radicals today, a point to which I shall return. Whether or not the point is valid, it is one with which serious educational theory must grapple, as the progressives did not.

It should be clear that to study the writing of leading educational theorists is not to learn what goes on in school. This has probably always been the case, and the progressive period is no exception. Did pedagogy change during the progressive period? If it did, did the impulse come from progressive theory or some other source? Historians, as I have pointed out, cannot answer these questions. They know that certain things happened—the introduction of industrial education, the kindergarten, and guidance; the development of ability grouping; the creation of "social studies"; the use in some places of movable furniture and the project method. But our knowledge, even about these tangible innovations, is vague. In how many places, for instance, was the project method used? What sorts of schools introduced guidance counselors first?

Even if we grant that a number of innovations entered schoolrooms and school systems, we still must ask about more fundamental issues. Had the attitudes of teachers altered? Was school in general a friendlier, happier place? Had there been an improvement in the relationship between the school and its community? I suspect the answers to these questions, when we learn them, will be negative. In fact, the significance of the changes that did occur is that they represent an outgrowth of long-standing concerns and well-established patterns, not new departures, and not the influence of progressive educational theory.

Consider, for instance, the introduction of industrial education. Relating the school to industrial employment had been a concern of many people, including employers' groups, for a long time. The argument that schooling was insuffici-

ently practical and that it paid too much attention to the head
and too little to the hand was not especially theoretical. For a
long time, though, advocates of directly vocational training
made little headway, and it was only toward the end of the
nineteenth century that they scored significant gains. The
timing of their success is suggestive; it coincides with both
heavy immigration and the increase in high school enrollment. It is possible to suppose that industrial education appeared to be a handy solution to the problem of catering to
large numbers of less able or less academic students. It was
also a solution fit for poor children; it would permit them to
attend secondary school without imbibing aspirations beyond
their class. It would continue to instill in them the attitudes
and skills appropriate to manual working-class status. Regardless of the rhetoric of its sponsors, industrial education has
proved to be an ingenious way of providing universal secondary schooling without disturbing the shape of the social
structure and without permitting excessive amounts of social
mobility.

A similar hypothesis accounts for the origin and spread of
the kindergarten. Early childhood education has a long history,
dating from the infant school movement in late-eighteenth-
century England. At that time philanthropists, concerned with
the problem of juvenile crime, urged the establishment of
schools for very young children, aged two or three. The purpose of such institutions was to counteract the unfavorable
moral environment of the home, which, it was argued, led to
delinquent and later criminal behavior. Although the infant
school movement failed to spread widely in America, its emphasis on early childhood education became a permanent feature of educational thought. Later schoolmen, including those
of the mid-nineteenth century, developed that emphasis. They,
too, stressed the importance of counteracting the unfavorable
influence of the home and argued that the primary purpose
of early education was the formation of attitudes rather than

the development of skills. It was this emphasis on the relationship of early childhood education to social order that fed the kindergarten movement, in the same way, quite obviously, that widespread concern with crime and welfare expenses have given impetus to movements for preschool education today.

Industrial education and the kindergarten represent outgrowths of the traditional conservative impulse at the basis of educational change. Other innovations, while reflecting that impulse as well, represent extensions of bureaucratic structure. These are ability grouping, the junior high school, and guidance. Each represented the introduction of one more specialized component into an increasingly subdivided, hierarchical form of organization. Each represented an extension of the already existing pattern of bureaucratic development, not a change of direction.

Guidance and ability grouping are also of interest because they too have functioned, despite their stated purposes, as social sorting devices. They have legitimized a way of channeling working-class children into working-class jobs; they have utilized the mantle of science to disguise the fact that schools reinforce existing patterns of social structure. Here the interrelationship between bureaucratic structure and class bias becomes especially clear. Bureaucracy provides a segmented educational structure that legitimizes and perpetuates the separation of children along class lines and ensures easier access to higher-status jobs for children of the affluent.

This is my hypothesis. The evidence to support it fully has not yet been compiled, but it is not inconsistent with the facts as they are known. It is a hypothesis about the function of educational innovations as distinct from their explicit purposes. It holds, in fact, that there is often a discrepancy between the two. As it relates to progressivism in education, the hypothesis maintains that most progressive innovations, so-called, operated as social sorting mechanisms supportive of existing social patterns and social inequalities. Despite the rhetoric of their sponsors, progressive innovations inhibited rather than fostered social change and social reform. Like the educational reform movement of the mid-nineteenth century, progressivism was profoundly conservative, for it sprang from a search for social order.

The attitudes of the men who directed educational change, city superintendents and professors of education, underlines the essentially conservative nature of progressivism. Once again, it is important to recall that historians have been remarkably slow about systematically studying the social attitudes of school administrators, but the little we do know suggests that they were strongly committed to bureaucratic forms and frequently racist in outlook. Certainly, the lessons that school administrators learned from the most eminent professors of education had conservative biases, as a study of the work of David Snedden, the virtual founder of educational sociology, or of Elwood Cubberly, a profoundly influential teacher of administration, reveals. Cubberly taught and wrote on the subject of administration and on educational history as well; his influence spread not only through those endeavors but also through the surveys of city school systems that he conducted. David Tyack has made it quite clear that Cubberly believed in the inferiority of new immigrant groups. Although Cubberly criticized school practice, his proposals for reform did not call as much for a change of structure or direction as for a more streamlined bureaucracy. What he proposed for the improvement of urban school systems was greater centralization, more professional control, and increased efficiency in operation.

An emphasis on efficiency permeated educational writing, and, indeed, reform writing in other fields as well, with monotonous regularity. Efficiency, as in the case examined earlier, continued to imply the application of scientific methods to simultaneously improve quality and lower costs. Raymond

Callahan has argued that the emphasis on efficiency, particularly scientific management, represented an almost conspiratorial attempt to foist business values on the school. That is stretching the point. It would be more accurate to say that the conduct of both social, including educational, reform and of business shared values that were prominent in American society, and that the men who ran schools differed little in their attitudes and outlook from the men who ran businesses. Whether an innovation appears to be progressive or regressive depends on the perspective of the observer. Thus, Lawrence Cremin considers the innovations in the schools of Gary, Indiana, to be the quintessence of progressivism, because they represented a wholehearted attempt to improve the practice of education within a city school system. Raymond Callahan, on the other hand, regards the Gary system as proof of the misapplication of scientific management in education because it represented an attempt to cut costs. Both historians are right, in a sense. Gary provides an excellent illustration of the dominant impulse of the period: the effort to obtain improvement and economy through the use of science.

If Robert and Helen Lynd were right and Middletown did represent a typical American city, then its educational history supports the arguments that I have advanced in this section. There, in the 1920's, the Lynds found an educational system virtually untouched by the theory and ferment of the preceding three decades. The school day in 1925 was rigid, dull, and routine, much as it must have been in 1890. In the intervening years the major changes had been the introduction of vocational courses, a heightened emphasis on the teaching of patriotism and civics, a blossoming of extracurricular activities, and the addition of more administrative personnel in the elaboration of the educational hierarchy. The school, however, remained, "like the factory," a "thoroughly regimented world." It was, in fact, in the 1930's, during the Depression, that the system changed most. The result of that change, to use Tyack's phrase, was a streamlined bureaucracy. The introduction of testing and guidance, the refinement of differences between schools, and of the professional self-consciousness of school people, the introduction of a research department, an assertion of the importance of individual differences, new curricula, an efficiency movement—these were some of the major changes. At the same time the expectations of the community remained the same, heightened, in fact, by the dislocations of the Depression. The schools were to continue to serve as a source of social order, stability, and the inculcation of patriotism. In short, Middletown's schools remained the same conservative, stabilizing institutions they had always been, now refurbished in modern form.

Progressive reforms touched Middletown late, and they touched it superficially. This was the usual course of events. Partly, the force of tradition, the resistance of educators to change, and the conservative expectations of communities all combined to frustrate educational reform. But that is not the entire story, as I hope this section has made clear. Progressive reform, even at its most articulate, did not challenge social or institutional structure. At its most typical it sought reforms profoundly congruent with the conservative commercial ethos at the heart of American life. Progressivism did not fail to work a fundamental transformation in American schools; it did not even try.

The Present Moment in Educational Reform

What of the current movement for educational reform? In what ways does it resemble those of the past? Is there any reason to believe that its results will be more fundamental? The parallels between the present and the past are implicit in what I have written so far. We are today experiencing the third major movement for urban educational reform in American history. Like those of the mid-nineteenth century and the progressive period, it is a part of a larger movement to improve the quality of urban life. But I use the present tense with some trepidation. For, as I write this, late in 1970, I think the drive and dynamism have gone. The indicator, as I pointed out earlier, was the re-emergence of emphasis on the role of heredity in educational achievement. Twice before, this kind of event signaled the waning of reformist energy; perhaps it has done so once again.

The current movement began partly with the traditional conservative concern about crime and social disorder on city streets; it intertwined with the thrust for civil rights, and the combination gave it, initially, enormous power. At the start, integration provided a great moral issue that united blacks, whites, liberals, radicals, and even many conservatives. That was early in the 1960's, and it seems now long ago, an arcadian era of wonderful simplicity. Two clear-cut goals emerged for education: improving urban schools, and ending *de facto* segregation. At the time they seemed to be possible, difficult but attainable. Compensatory education and integration provided the means with which reform began; it was a moment of great optimism. Since that time the tensions inherent in the movement have erupted. The strains and contradictions between integration and compensatory education, between integration and decentralization, and between radical pedagogical reform and community participation—these, to name but three, have driven wedges into the movement, fragmenting it into antagonistic pieces.

The parallels between the four models presented earlier and contemporary proposals for reform are striking. The least explicit is paternalistic voluntarism, but it is nonetheless present, underlying the idea that school boards should be formed of a small body of first citizens appointed by the mayor. The proposal rests, first, on the naive assumption, characteristic also of paternalistic voluntarists, that education can somehow be divorced from politics. It rests, too, on the familiar and elitist premise that there resides within the community a body of disinterested and wise citizens, devoid of political or personal motives, uniquely capable of identifying and implementing the public interest in education.

Corporate voluntarism has become a widely discussed alternative during the last few years. Its contemporary sponsors, such as Christopher Jencks, propose the replacement of the public monopoly of schooling with competing private groups operating their own institutions. The voucher system represents a popular version of this idea; its sponsors want to replace the direct funding of public schools with educational vouchers, financed, as now, by taxation, but cashable by parents or students at any school. Their model is classic liberal economics; the argument is that free competition among schools will foster quality education and that the fight for funds will produce both a variety of school types and a continuing effort to offer an education that is attractive to its customers. The contemporary proponents of corporate voluntarism argue that their proposals would put flexibility, variety, and a stimulus to improvement back into the conduct of education.

As in the mid-nineteenth century, democratic localism today is the most disputed alternative. Its advocates—for instance, in Ocean Hill–Brownsville—are the champions of community control; they propose the radical decentralization of city school systems into small districts governed by local community organizations. Their values are not dissimilar to those of Orestes Brownson; like him, they stress the virtues of a close relationship between school and community, the drawbacks of bureaucracy, and the relation of community control to democratic theory. They, too, distrust professionals. They seek a redistribution of power from the interests represented by central city governments to the poor and, in the case of ghetto people, to the black community itself. The search for black control of black institutions, especially schools, underlies much of the drive for community control. In this, too, there is a parallel between the present situation and the effort of the Irish Catholics in New York City to decentralize that city's system in the 1840's in order to gain control of the funds and institutions that provided schooling for their children.

Incipient bureaucracy likewise has its contemporary echoes. It might be more accurate, today, to speak of incipient technocracy. This variety of educational reform seeks to make changes within the existing educational system; it proposes sophisticated technological innovations to improve the content and procedures of schooling. Its most visible symbol is computer-assisted instruction. It is a point of view that does not feel uneasy about size; in fact, its proponents often advocate the creation of large educational parks that can economically incorporate the most advanced features of educational technology. Like the incipient bureaucrats of the last century, the technocrats stress the efficiency of their proposals and the increase in educational cost-benefit ratios that they will achieve. They likewise emphasize the importance of professionalism and the creation of new specialist roles within school systems. This approach to reform receives powerful support from two sources. One is from integrationists, who argue that only large educational parks drawing from a wide residential area can overcome the problem of *de facto* segregation based on housing. The other is professors of education; many support this approach, which assigns increased status and importance to their work and provides a justification for increased research funds.

With the exception of the technocrats, the proposals for reform that I have outlined stress structural changes, particularly the need to alter the political basis of educational control. In this there is an apparent similarity between the strivings of contemporary reformers and those of the progressive period. However, the direction of the movement is different today. The progressives, as we have seen, tried to centralize education; the main thrust of contemporary radical reform is toward decentralization. Two assumptions of the present movement deserve special attention. The first is that political change must precede educational change—that it is necessary to alter the political control of the school system before anything meaningful can change within the classroom. Second is the expectation that political change, meaning here the introduction of community control, will foster pedagogical reform; that it will mean children will receive a better education.

It is important to emphasize these assumptions because they, in turn, highlight the extent to which the movement for community control rests on particular value premises. It rests partly on the value that some black people attach to control of the education their children receive. Education controlled by whites, or reflecting white attitudes, they argue, by virtue of that fact cannot be adequate for black children. The other value position is the inherent worth that community control finds in close, almost symbiotic relations between institutions and the communities they serve. Community control, as much as earlier forms of educational organization, is a crystallization of certain values and priorities. Technocracy, for instance, gives priority to efficiency in terms of time and money, the attainment of intellectual skills, and professionalism. At one level, therefore, the differences between reform proposals are irreconcilable.

That is an important point, which contemporary debate obscures. Only some of the points at issue are open to discussion. Reformers, from one perspective, waste time talking to each other; they should put their proposals before the public, which eventually will have to choose between competing organizational forms and the values that they enshrine. Polemics, however, have only limited use; it would be more productive for proponents of differing viewpoints to identify the aspects of each other's positions that can in fact be challenged and discussed. The technocrats, for example, might ask the democrats to provide evidence that a change in the source of educational control will improve the content of schooling. The latter, in turn, might ask their antagonists to demonstrate the value of professionalism in education by, say, showing how graduate instruction in school administration improves the quality of education. Is there a relationship between the amount of graduate instruction given a school principal and the level at which the students in his school read and write?

One of the problems of contemporary reform is that people talk past each other, or else only to those already converted. The amount of good dialogue remains small. A second problem is the failure of the political and educational left honestly and hard-headedly to confront the value conflicts inherent within their own position. The left has become, in fact, tragically polarized, as the New York teachers' strike of 1968 demonstrated. The result has been dogmatic refusal to admit the ambiguities and contradictions within each position. One must, for instance, be either for or against community control. To be against, or to qualify one's comments, has come to be racist, an epithet that is clearly absurd if applied to men of unquestionably humane and democratic convictions, like Michael Harrington, who spoke on the side of the teachers.

It is not my intention to recount the events of the New York teachers strike or to try to untangle the web of charges and countercharges made by each side. There is ample documentation elsewhere, enough for readers to draw their own conclusions; I refer anyone interested, for a start, to Marilyn Gittell and Maurice Berube, *Confrontation at Ocean Hill–Brownsville*. I bring up the strike primarily to illustrate the dilemmas posed by community control, which supporters must confront but which, as I have said, are more obscured than dissected at present.

First of all, there is the problem of the teacher as a professional. In the early 1960's teacher unionism was a favorite cause with angry young graduate students in education and other educational radicals. These are the very people who today are among its strongest critics. But the arguments advanced in the early 1960's retain their validity. Teaching in America has always been poorly paid and poorly regarded. It is only recently that teachers have gained some measure of employment security and freedom from harassment and dismissal at the whim of school boards. Dreadful working conditions combined with the lack of autonomy, status, and adequate pay have sent people away from teaching in droves; it is a commonplace to observe that the brightest university graduates have not often entered the schools. Teacher unionism has been a response, and a very constructive one, to that problem.

Autonomy has been central to the problem. Even people who have been willing to accept a poor salary and who can remain indifferent to status have been repelled by the lack of autonomy, the rigid and petty authoritarian ethos of the schools. Bright, creative, and well-educated people want to function as professionals, to make the decisions about how they will do their job. Education has not suffered from any freedom granted teachers to run schools as they see fit; it has suffered from the suffocating atmosphere in which teachers have had to work. The popular attitude, and even that of reformers, equates the aims of administrators with those of teachers; it blames teachers for bureaucracy. The important point is that a distinction must be made; teachers do not run the schools. They are, as they will often tell you, harassed by the administration, which, if they are any good, continually gets in their way.

We have never had the situation in schools that we have in universities, where the faculty makes the educational decisions. Any attempted interference by governing boards with curriculum or pedagogy is greeted by academics, and justifiably, with appeals to academic freedom. In light of this, it is ironical, to say the least, that academics should support community control, at least as it has been advocated in Ocean

Hill–Brownsville, quite so uncritically. For, according to its by-laws, the governing board there retained to itself absolute power over all activities within the schools. What kind of educational change can be accomplished by exchanging one arbitrary educational authority for another?

It is ironical, too, that the teachers have opposed community control so uncreatively. They have sought not their freedom but their shelter in the protection of the bureaucracy. This, of course, reinforces the radical stereotype of the teacher as a rule-following servant of authority. On the radicals' side, too, is the unquestioned fact that many teachers are hostile to children, racist, or incompetent. Such teachers should be fired; they deserve no protection and no place in schools. Their protection by their colleagues and by the bureaucracy constitutes an enormous indictment of both.

It would be in the interests of both teachers and communities to develop a modified concept of decentralization and community school control. That concept would call for radically decentralized schools, each run by a coalition of teachers, parents, and students, much as the most progressive reformers are proposing for the restructuring of universities. Sensible divisions of authority, leaving to the teachers wide areas in which to exercise professional judgment, could be found. This sort of arrangement would offer the teachers the freedom to become professionals, which they now lack; it might also help to attract some independent-minded persons into teaching. It would offer communities decentralized schools and a meaningful role in their conduct. Students would gain the place in educational decision-making that they deserve, and the bureaucracy could be made obsolete. There would still be an important function for a teachers' union and equally, I think, for a union of students, who need to have their rights protected as well.

This is a straightforward way out of one of the conflicts that has troubled the decentralization movement (although I do not expect it would be easy to persuade the teachers' union to accept it). The other conflict appears to me less easy to resolve: the problem of integration. Community control and integration are incompatible, and for anyone who wants both that is a very hard fact to admit. Decentralized community schools must of necessity be small and local. In cities, that means that they must be within the ghettos; segregated residential patterns make it impossible for it to be otherwise. Nevertheless, integration is not impossible, as a number of people have argued; metropolitan cooperation in the creation of large educational parks could bring it about. Educational parks, however, would have to be large and formal, tightly administered, and distant from the communities they serve. At their best, they would be highly centralized, superlatively efficient, technologically advanced bureaucracies. They would decrease the possibilities of flexibility, variety, and community involvement. At their worst, they would be dreadful prisons, large repressive institutions with all the faults of contemporary urban schools magnified.

The Coleman report complicates the situation. It points, first, to the enormous disparity between white and black educational achievement. The median arithmetic score for black children graduating grade twelve is sixth grade. Reading is somewhat, but not much, better. Black and white children begin school not too far apart in test scores, but over time black scores fall and the differential increases. Part, and a very large part, of that cripplingly low educational achievement can be improved by integration; children segregated by social class or by race do much worse than those in integrated settings. Despite the weaknesses of the Coleman report, one finding appears undeniable: We could increase the educational achievement of black children substantially by sending them to schools in which a majority of the children are white. The same thing—and this is important, for it has the same implications for community control—is true of poor or lower-class children, despite their color. If they are sent to schools with a majority of middle-class students, their performance will improve. Moreover, it is not only academic achievement that will improve. The Coleman data show a substantial improvement in racial attitudes among students in integrated schools. White children who go to school with black children are more accepting, less racist, than those of comparable intelligence and status who attend all-white schools. Integration appears, then, to be a way to attack racist attitudes.

It is difficult, if not impossible, to conceive of a way of arranging schooling that permits integration, small size, and deep community involvement. That is the dilemma. Even if the goal of integration is abandoned—as it seems increasingly to be, with the sanction of both blacks and whites, though of course for different reasons—even in that case the problem of educational achievement remains. Reading and mathematics are skills that black children must learn as well as white and that in fact they do not now learn, for reasons that lie more within the school setting, it would appear, than within their homes. For, it seems to me, the Coleman data also suggest that the retarding influence of "impoverished" homes has been grossly overrated. Put in an integrated school context— that is, one more conducive to learning—black children and poor white children, regardless of their home background, achieve more. The Coleman report, it has been pointed out frequently, measures only the learning that takes place within fairly traditional classroom settings. It is entirely possible that radically different educational contexts or procedures will enable black or poor children to learn more readily in schools that are *not* integrated. But two qualifications must be considered: Within a broad range of standard educational practice, the Coleman report indicates that differences in educational facilities, such as pupil-teacher ratio or per-pupil expenditure, do not matter much. Secondly, reanalysis of the Coleman data and of the report *Racial Isolation in the Public Schools* shows that programs of compensatory education, programs that aim at improving the educational achievement of black children within segregated ghetto schools, have not worked despite heavy funding.

At best, we can remain hopeful, but realistically we must admit that what we know in any hard-headed way is that we are not certain how to improve the educational achievement of black or poor children where they go to school only with each other; we do know that we can improve their achievement by sending them to integrated schools, and we know as well that we can decrease racial bias in the process. We must remember, though, that integration implies increased centralization. It calls for an increase in those very characteristics of educational structure against which much contemporary reform has been directed, and justly so. One of the greatest weaknesses of education has been its bureaucratic form of organization; integration will only make that form more permanent. For advocates of both decentralization and integration, and I count myself among them, the future appears very bleak.

Educational radicals often fail to appreciate another dilemma, which the following incident illustrates. Seven poor mothers, disgusted with the treatment of their children in special classes for slow learners, began a little school of their own. Located in a vacant slum house, it had ten children taught by four undergraduates from a local university. When it came time to elect members for the city school board, the mothers decided that one of their number stand.

To plan the campaign they called on volunteers from the university and from a political party. At campaign meetings in the schoolhouse, the mothers sat on one side of the room, projecting anger at a school system that, they felt, ignored and insulted them and their children. On the other side sat the outsiders, dressed mostly in casual clothes, with longish hair, who saw in the mothers an indigenous community movement representing educational radicalism and participatory democracy. Pressed by the outsiders, the mothers offered personal stories of educational injustice, but very few specific educational objectives. When the candidate did adopt a platform, she advocated the reintroduction of report cards and corporal punishment; she opposed sex education.

The gulf that opened between the candidate and her imported supporters underlines the romantic fantasy at the core of much educational radicalism. For it expects a humanitarian and libertarian revolution in education to accompany a shift in power from the bureaucracy to the people. There are two distinguishable major strands in contemporary educational radicalism. One concentrates on the compulsory and bureaucratic structure of education, which it seeks to alter through the creation of alternatives to public schooling or through the redistribution of educational power to local communities within cities. This is the strand we have been considering. Another focuses on the spirit-breaking quality of current administrative and pedagogical practices and stresses the liberation of both teacher and student. Just as advocates of the former care more for community involvement than for administrative efficiency, the latter put happiness and warm human relations above subjects, skills, and classroom order.

It would be wrong to separate the two too sharply. Most educational radicals whose work I have read espouse both positions; the difference is a matter of emphasis. In fact, there is a premise, which we have noticed before, that the liberation of pedagogy will follow the liberation of the educational structure. It is clear, however, as the anecdote presented above demonstrates, that the two goals, pedagogical and political-structural, do not coexist in the minds of the constituency to which educational radicals appeal.

Nevertheless, despite—or perhaps because of—its visionary streak, the educational radicalism of the last several years has provided a beautiful, moving, and right-hearted body of pedagogical literature. The most effective of the radicals to me are experienced, deeply committed teachers who sensitively distill the history of their involvement with schools: I think of Sylvia Ashton-Warner, George Dennison, and A. S. Neill as examples. They are romantic about human potentiality and about education, and they are vulnerable as well to the logic-chopping ax of the academic critic. But that is irrelevant, for they are great teachers. And it is their presence, which manages to survive print, rather than any specific suggestion of method, that gives their writing its lucidity and inspiration. Educational radicalism gains its strength as well from the conditions it describes. Its proposals can be debated, but its critique is generally hard to fault; the school conditions that radicals attack are already appalling, as the film *High School* shows even more vividly than Jonathan Kozol's description of human destruction in the Boston schools.

The problem that educational radicalism as a critique now faces is how to maintain its urgency and driving force, for it is becoming popular, and its leading tenets, sometimes in distorted form, are expressed by a wide variety of people. At the mercy of lesser people, educational radicalism, like progressivism in an earlier era, rigidifies into a new orthodoxy that is nearly as dry and gutless as the old. Its history, I fear, will fall into the pattern cut earlier in the century by progressive educational thought, which, as a moment in intellectual history, combined an emphasis on community with a desire to liberate the child. In practice, though, as I have noted earlier, progressivism often added only a set of new wrinkles to an already overdeveloped educational bureaucracy. Rather than liberate the child from scholasticism, repression, and drill, the discovery of individual differences, as an instance, fueled the development of massive psychological testing and the creation of the guidance bureaucracy stretching from school counselors to university departments. Similarly, the professor of educational administration remains a more permanent artifact of the progressive era than Dewey's laboratory school. It was administrative values—the addition of supervisory positions, the war on inefficiency, the introduction of ability grouping—rather than the promotion of social reform through the democratic liberation of human intelligence, that most often defined the progressive spirit in practice.

Contemporary radicalism, in fact, may already be recapitulating the progressive experience. Here the Province of Ontario provides an especially clear example, with relevance for Americans as well as Canadians.

Not long ago, a provincial commission on the aims and objectives of education published a multicolored, illustrated, and self-consciously progressive report entitled *Living and Learning* (known locally as the Hall-Dennis report). It is a remarkable document and a shiny testament to the impact of educational radicalism. In it the representatives of the provincial Establishment, from whom the membership of the committee was drawn, declare themselves unequivocally in favor of child-centered schools for all; the reorganization of the curriculum into thematic, interdisciplinary components; and the virtual abandonment of age-grading throughout the school system. It is an official document simply unthinkable prior to the late 1960's.

Yet *Living and Learning*, despite its genuine obeisance to contemporary educational thought, remains a tame and essentially safe document (fit product of a Tory government), which never questions basic premises. It not only accepts compulsory education but intimates that its extension may become desirable; it fails to explore the existence of alternatives to public education; and, tellingly, it unquestioningly accepts traditional class-linked notions. One such notion, to which we should be alert by now, is the concept of cultural deprivation, a fancy way of labeling the lower orders inferior or, as I have observed above, depraved, in nineteenth-century terms. Another is the emphasis on the development of desirable (whose definition is no more specified now than in the time of Horace Mann) attitudes, which historically, of course, has meant the reformation of working-class morals according to the image in an idealized middle-class mirror. For all its progressive finish, alas, *Living and Learning* ducks the questions that matter most. At best it is castrated educational radicalism.

Living and Learning, I suspect, is the harbinger of a new progressivism that aspires to the radical mantle. That the movement will not deserve that distinction is hardly surprising. From the most cynical point of view, it is an old and usually brilliant trick of school people, like any bureaucrats, to dilute the strength of an attack by appearing to adopt the language of the enemy. Beyond that, however, there are weaknesses within educational radicalism itself, which have not been fully explored, and these bring us back to the story with which I began this section.

Educational radicalism has been offered as a cure for the pathology afflicting the education of the urban poor. But the mother from the slums whom I mentioned earlier may be more representative of the attitudes of poor people, than, say, Paul Goodman is. In fact, I suspect that what the poor want for their children is affluence, status, and a house in the suburbs rather than community, a guitar, and soul. They may prefer schools that teach their children to read and write and cipher rather than to feel and to be. If this is the case, then an uncomfortable piece of reality must be confronted: Educational radicalism is itself a species of class activity. It reflects an attempt at cultural imposition fully as much as the traditional educational emphasis on competition, restraint, and orderliness, whose bourgeois bias radicals are quick to excoriate.

There is a pathetic lack of fit between the poor and the schools, but educational radicalism offers us as much an ideology as a solution. Since the early nineteenth century, nostalgic intellectuals (like the democratic localists discussed earlier), frustrated by the scale and impersonality of urban life, have flirted recurrently with a vision of democratic, communally controlled, humanistic education. But factionalism, bigotry, and narrowness marked nineteenth-century rural towns at least as often as democratic communalism. If the racism in Cairo, Illinois, the persecution of teachers who discussed the United Nations in southern California, and the advocacy of report cards and corporal punishment by the indigenous candidate from the slums are at all representative, they suggest that people have changed very little, and that in turn should give pause to contemporary radicals.

All this is not meant to suggest that the radical critique of education is unfounded. It is profoundly true. Frighteningly often, schools destroy education and, more important, children. Unfortunately, a broadly acceptable alternative remains to be found. I doubt that we shall see an alternative soon, for educational radicalism already has become a new orthodoxy. Proof of that is *Radical School Reform*, a recent anthology of writings by contemporary radicals edited by Ronald and Beatrice Gross. It is a good anthology, for it represents the movement fairly, and it has thematic unity. But that is the point: The orthodoxy inheres in the success with which the movement can be anthologized and in the predictability of the Grosses' table of contents. The names there, ones we have heard again and again, are in fact those of the priests of the movement. In the last analysis, the anthology signals that educational radicalism has passed from a sect to a church. In the process it has lost its sting.

Four Suggestions for Reformers

This book has been an essay in historical social criticism; its tone has been largely negative. For that I think no apology is needed. Despite all that has been written on the ills of urban education, little has been said that helps to put those problems into a proper perspective by showing the development of the patterns and the establishment of the processes that have formed city school systems. The main difficulty with the traditional pietistic version of educational history is that it simply does not account for the schools that we now have. It is like the pietistic, conflict-free version of American history that would leave us today, were it true, amid a prospering, progressive, and consensual society marked by a happy, tolerant pluralism and equality for all men. We all know the real truth about society, and about schools as well. The purpose of this book has been to connect the history of the latter with that reality.

However, all this said, there are four positive suggestions for reformers that emerge from this analysis. The first relates to the purposes of education. It must be emphasized that, opinion to the contrary notwithstanding, people ask no more of schools today than they did a hundred and twenty-five years ago. Even then the schools were asked to do the impossible. As we have seen, the purpose of the school people has been more the development of attitudes than of intellect, and this continues to be the case. It is true, and this point must be stressed, of radical reformers as well as of advocates of law and order. The latter want the schools to stop crime and check immorality by teaching obedience to authority, respect for the law, and conformity to conventional standards. The former want the schools to reform society by creating a new sense of community through turning out warm, loving, noncompetitive people.

The human qualities that radical reformers seek in and through the schools are very beautiful ones; if achieved, they would give us a worthier and lovelier society. But it is no more realistic to charge the schools with the creation of such qualities than it is to expect them to fulfill traditional moralistic aims. Whatever values one attaches to the counterculture, whatever interpretation one gives to social conflict and crime, it is clear that the powers of schooling have been vastly overrated. Despite substantial financing and a captive audience, the schools have not been able to attain the goals set for them, with remarkably little change, for the last century and a quarter. They have been unable to do so because those goals have been impossible to fulfill. They require fundamental social reform, not the sort of tinkering that educational change has represented. If, by some miracle, the radical reformers were to capture the schools, and only the schools, for the next century, they would have no more success than educational reformers of the past.

The moral should be clear. Educational reformers should begin to distinguish between what formal schooling can and cannot do. They must separate the teaching of skills from the teaching of attitudes, and concentrate on the former. In actual fact, it is of course impossible to separate the two; attitudes adhere in any form of practice. But there is a vast difference between leaving the formation of attitudes untended and making them the object of education.

This is a radical position, despite the ordinary presumption to the contrary. In the popular version, schools once upon a time concentrated on the three R's. With no nonsense and remarkable success, they taught children to read, write, cipher, and spell. Then along came progressivism, which turned the schools into a combination social-service and life-adjustment bureau, forgetting, in the process, all about training in skills and the importance of the intellect. That history is simply false. The denigration of intellect and the neglect of skills have been continuing features of the history of public education; early school promoters believed quite as much as progressives that they were creating institutions to alleviate and prevent social problems.

There is a lot of talk about the foisting of middle-class values onto working-class children through the schools. In fact that happens to be an oversimplification, as Paul Goodman has pointed out beautifully in *Compulsory Mis-educa-*

tion. The values taught by the schools are not the tough, ascetic historic values of the bourgeois. Be that as it may, although schools do confront children with values that may be different from their own or from those of their parents, attempting to reverse the case may not prove desirable either, for the values of the poor may be those of the woman from the slum that I described earlier. The way out of this problem, it seems to me, is once again to take the schools out of the business of making attitudes. Have them attend to skills, especially, in the beginning, reading, and the question of whose values control the schools becomes largely irrelevant. For it is my premise that the desire that children become functionally literate and able to understand mathematics is nearly universal; it is as true of poor as of affluent parents.

To talk of cultural deprivation is to patronize the poor; it also is to deflect effort away from the education that they need. Poor children need to learn to read, not to visit museums, and I have seen no evidence of a correlation between the two. People have a right to hold whatever beliefs and whatever attitudes they please; that is the only consistent position for a civil libertarian. It follows that the attempt in schools to define one set of attitudes as superior to another, the attempt to teach patriotism, conventional morality, or even its opposite in a *compulsory* public institution represents a gross violation of civil rights.

My point is that educational theory should define strictly educational tasks and that schools should concentrate on those. Any such definition must include, at one end of the spectrum, fundamental skills; at the other, it must exclude the conscious attempt to formulate social attitudes. I am not arguing for what has been traditional in much educational practice; mental gymnastics for their own sake or the forced study of useless disciplines is indefensible. So is the rigid, authoritarian atmosphere of most schools. Schools should be made open, humane places for the simple reason that children have every right to be happy and to be treated with dignity and respect.

The atmosphere of the school relates to my second thought for reformers. The reformulation of educational purposes cannot be accomplished within current educational structures. Bureaucracy, as I hope I have made clear, is more than a form of organization; it is the crystallization of particular values. Through their structures, schools communicate a purpose; for contemporary schools, Robert Dreeben, in *On What Is Learned in Schools*, has made that very clear. School structure communicates particular norms; the learning of those norms has priority to the learning of skills. Those norms that are crystallized into contemporary educational forms reflect the purposes of education that have dominated American schools. Any radical reformulation of educational objectives, it follows, requires a radical restructuring of educational forms.

It is difficult to see the functional relationships between large size, economies of scale, bureaucratic organization, and so on, on the one hand, and learning to read, write, and do math, on the other. Unless the effectiveness of electronic computers proves revolutionary at these tasks (which I doubt), it is hard to see why the business of learning these things cannot be managed more simply, directly, and informally by skilled teachers working with small groups of children wherever they can find some space. The public can provide the equipment and materials and pay the salaries and rent, as now, but the activities do not have to be carried on within what we now call a school. The setting can be warm, colorful, comfortable, and humane without being expensive. Perhaps in some instances children need special facilities and special teachers, as in art, music, or history; perhaps even at an early age they should have access to laboratories for science. These facilities should be very good indeed. Children could go to them as they need and want to. It is not my intention to offer a detailed plan here. Rather, I just wish to emphasize what seems to me a very commonsensical position. Let us examine each of the activities children will undertake as they grow up and ask how it might best be handled, best in the sense of economy, of humaneness, of making the setting a happy one. In the process, we should avoid large institutions, bureaucratic organization, and complexity whenever anything else will serve as well.

It would be well if this reformed set of educational arrangements could be voluntary; compulsion should be removed on principle, wherever possible. However, and this is my third suggestion, the abolition of compulsion should be accompanied by radical changes in educational structure; it may be dangerous for children if it happens alone. Consider for a moment the possibilities inherent in abolishing compulsory schooling without making any other major social or educational changes. Parents might pressure children to leave school early in order to go to work; employers would exploit juvenile labor. We offer at present little worthwhile work to a young person uninterested in formal schooling, and, what is of most importance of all, we do not offer alternative ways of becoming educated or easy access back into schooling. Given the present rigid, sequential, age-graded system, the young person who leaves school early and later wants to re-enter faces major problems. Abolishing compulsory education could work against the interests of all children, especially the poor, if it were not accompanied by provisions to enable them to find worthwhile work and to resume formal education with financial support whenever they want to do so. The connection between level of schooling and employment opportunity will have to be broken as well, as it should be. All these things should be done. As Paul Goodman has argued, we must permit alternative ways for people to grow and to live. That is the real purpose of abolishing compulsory education. Otherwise, we might simply serve the needs of industry in search of cheap labor or of taxpayers whose only interest is lowering educational cost.

The same caution about balance applies to decentralization. My fourth suggestion is the point I made earlier: Decentralization should include a shift of power to teachers and students, away from administrators, as well as to local communities. Many of the recommendations for community control represent merely the exchange of one arbitrary governing authority for another. It is certainly true that parents could hardly do a worse job of running ghetto schools than educational bureaucracies have done. When the median math score of twelfth-grade children is grade six, it is impossible to argue with any honesty that community control will hurt educational achievement. But that is not enough. For decentralization to bring about improvements, the teacher as well as the school must be liberated.

There is no one way, nor even a few ways, of rightly arranging for education. There are many ways, and anyone who argues otherwise is foolish. Most arrangements should have, perhaps, certain features, and I have suggested some of them. But, for the most part, the particular form education should take in any one place should be worked out by the people involved. Professional educationists can offer a great deal of assistance, but the days when they should offer blueprints have ended. Let us be thankful, for that system has brought us to where we are: Too many children do not learn well and are unhappy in school; teachers suffer and lack autonomy; parents are dissatisfied; and economists warn of impending massive unemployment. Not even a college degree assures one a job any more. Aside from the people who live off the education system, and I do not mean the teachers, it has served no one very well. We are all its victims, and no one has done very much constructive about that for the last century. I should like to think that the time has come.

Epilogue: Education, Reform, and American History—An Exchange*

I

As its critics have observed, this little book is far from perfect, and, indeed, the generosity with which most reviewers have received it has surprised and delighted me. Here I wish neither to be defensive nor to respond to the occasional points of misinterpretation or misreading in some reviews. Rather, I wish to comment on ten of the most important critical remarks that have been made about the book. My purpose is to clarify some issues that the book quite obviously leaves dangling ambiguously and to highlight a few of the major areas of unresolved controversy on which research and debate might center. I shall take up most of these points in greater detail in the commentaries on recent work in the field which follow. However, it seems useful to gather them together at the beginning as well.

The first, a minor point, concerns the four models of organization outlined in Chapter 1, which some critics argue are more aptly described as ideal types than my discussion ad-

---

* Portions and somewhat different versions of three of the essays in this Epilogue have been published elsewhere: "The Origins of Urban Education," *Reviews in American History* II, No. 2 (June 1974): 186–92; review of *Roots of Crisis, Harvard Educational Review* XLIII, No. 3 (May, 1973): 435–42; review of *Crisis in the Classroom, Interchange* III, No. 1 (1972): 96–101.

mitted. Though their point is well taken, the models are no less important or expressive of social values than I contended. A second criticism has been that my argument in Chapter 3 understates the amount of educational change that took place in the twentieth century. This criticism represents, I think, some misinterpretation of my argument, and I shall address it directly in my discussion of Marvin Lazerson's *Origins of the Urban School.*

Third, Carl Kaestle and Marvin Lazerson * imply that I have minimized both the role of individuals acting either alone or collectively as school boards and the accidental, messy nature of much historical development. That, too, probably represents a valid observation about this book, though not about my conception of history. For I have tried in the case study of the Boston system and in case studies published elsewhere to show something of the complex process through which educational change occurred in different contexts. However, it is true that this book quite deliberately highlights general developments. I wanted to argue that what happened represented more than a series of haphazard events emerging from countless decisions by local school boards, that patterns displayed in various places across the country looked remarkably alike and served quite similar purposes. Unless one retains an unshakable faith in coincidence, this strikes me as compelling evidence for general forces and processes, which we must try to discover and comprehend.

Fourth, and a related issue, Kaestle has made the important and certainly valid observation that people create structures which they inject with their own racism or class bias. The danger for the social scientist is the reification of those

* Carl Kaestle, "Social Reform and the Urban School," *History of Education Quarterly* 12, No. 1 (Summer, 1972): 211–28, and Marvin Lazerson, "Revisionism and American Educational History," *Harvard Educational Review* 43 (May, 1973): 270–83.

structures. A school system, after all, is not an animate, breathing organism. It is set of buildings, rules, relationships, equipment, and people. Nonetheless, as people create systems that embody their aspirations and beliefs, as they shape structures to reach certain ends, they incorporate from the beginning such features as racism and class bias. Thus the question becomes: Can a structure be made to serve very different goals from those that it was constructed, successfully, to reach? That is the question I have asked in this book. My inclination is to answer it pessimistically; but I could be, and in this case would be happy to be, wrong.

Fifth, although the infererence of some critics is incorrect that I find reformers of the past mean and nasty, I agree that my treatment of their motivation is far from satisfactory. Most of the misunderstanding has come, very likely, from the evasiveness with which I have treated the question. The only defense is that the interpretation of motivation in the analysis of reform remains generally inadequate (a point upon which I shall elaborate later).

Sixth, as Kaestle points out, this book may be misleading in another way: It is possible to take from my discussion the erroneous impression that I believe the schools to have been an unqualified failure. Aside from the question of their success in teaching particular skills or subjects, my point is that the schools failed to serve the poor or to reform society in the ways in which their sponsors predicted. Schools did not alleviate poverty and crime, significantly alter social structure, or make American society noticeably more democratic. On the other hand, the schools probably have been successful in serving the interests of the social classes that encouraged their establishment and subsequent development. There is a good deal of evidence to show that moderately prosperous people sought concrete advantages from school systems: They wanted schools to help their children to retain or improve their status; they sought a relatively inexpensive set of institutions to contain their children during an adolescence in which employment was no longer customary; they wished to preserve the distribution of power and resources that existed, permitting just enough social mobility to bolster the expanding, changing economy and to assure social peace. Schools have served these purposes magnificently, cloaking them in a convincing, if distorted, democratic rhetoric. It is probably a fact that societies get the schools they want. That, in the last analysis, is the most depressing observation I can offer about American education and American life.

Seventh, some women readers have pointed out, quite correctly, that I do not discuss the sex bias in American education. It is a measure of the success of the women's movement in affecting public consciousness over the last four or five years that I could not write the book today without attention to the way in which sexual, as much as class and race, bias has marked the structure of educational systems since their inception. I can only hope that other historians will remedy this deficiency in the book. Indeed, there already exist strong indications that the deplorable inattention to the role of women in American education is being overcome.

The eighth criticism is one I find hard to answer, for it often reflects a different political perspective from my own. It is the contention that my perspective on contemporary affairs has distorted my interpretation of the past. As most critics have recognized, I tried to make my biases explicit rather than mask them with a neutrality that I cannot feel. But, of course, that is no excuse for sloppy thinking, and I have worried much over the extent to which my point of view may have led me to misread or misinterpret what happened a century ago. Usually, it is asserted that I distort either by passing an unduly harsh judgment on the events and people in educational history, a point I have mentioned already, or by drawing parallels that ignore the differences between past and present. It would be foolhardy to deny the existence of fundamental differences of context between centuries, or even between situations only decades apart. The misuse of historical parallels, in fact, can be fatal, as the application of the domino theory to Southeast Asia should have shown for all time. Still, continuities and, I believe, certain kinds of cycles do exist. I have chosen to highlight the striking echoes of earlier themes in contemporary educational reform because they reflect important continuities in the relationship between formal education and society. These continuities offer a corrective to the evolutionary assumptions of most educational history and conventional wisdom. They underscore the difficulty of innovation and the unresolved dilemmas of reform. Those are lessons worth stressing.

A ninth criticism takes issue with the guidelines for reformers in the last chapter, the most speculative and least substantial part of the book. This chapter has received too much attention. Indeed, when I have spoken publicly about the book, most questions and criticisms have centered on this last chapter, especially on my advocacy of literacy and cognitive skills as the basic goals of early schooling. This is unfortunate; the heart of the book lies elsewhere, and my proposals are offered modestly, not as concrete programs but as some guidelines to which history, if it has a moral, appears to point. I know, of course (and, contrary to what some critics have implied, it is stated in the text), that no pedagogical method or subject matter is value-free. But there is an important distinction between educational experiences that take moral uplift as their primary goal and those that pursue intellectual development. And my contention (to which I shall return in my discussion of Charles Silberman's *Crisis in the Classroom*) is that in the history of American education moral purposes have always been more compelling than intellectual ones.

Finally, I should not like my position on the relation of the schools to social reform to be misunderstood. In the *New York Review of Books* Christopher Lasch concluded quite wrongly that my neo-Progressivism left me with the familiar fallacy of expecting the schools to initiate social reform. That is not only an erroneous reading of the book; it is quite the opposite message from that which I intended to convey. Schools exist as part of a social system. Meaningful change can come to that system only through a redistribution of power and resources. In that redistributive process schools can play a negligible role at best. By and large, the inequities of American education are the inequities of American society. And, though we can make schools much happier places for students and teachers, we cannot readily alter their social role. I expect, for instance, that any serious effort to equip poor children as effective competitors for the well-to-do will meet enormous, and probably successful, resistance. At this juncture, then, the contribution of the history of education to social reform remains mainly negative: The schools, it should by now be clear, are not the place to begin the task of changing society. Though negative, that lesson should not be undervalued, for it is a fundamental and necessary corrective to a national myth.

II

Two recent books—*The Evolution of an Urban School System*, by Carl Kaestle, and *The Culture Factory*, by Stanley Schultz *—reinforce the lesson that schools proved inadequate to alleviate the social distress they had been created to contain. Through a detailed discussion of developments in New York and Boston, respectively, these books illustrate the process described abstractly in the first chapter of this book. Although neither author would agree with me completely, their analyses, I believe, strengthen and support the general interpretation of the origins of public education I have of-

* Full references to these and other works discussed in this Epilogue are given in the section headed "A Note on Sources, Personal and Otherwise" at the end of the text, under "Addendum: August, 1974."

fered. Where we all would admit agreement, certainly, is on the essentially conservative purposes of early education; on the fear of poverty, delinquency, and cultural heterogeneity that impelled school reform. We would agree, too, about the drive toward system and bureaucracy that underlay the passionate public school crusades of the early and mid-nineteenth century.

Between the late eighteenth and the mid-nineteenth centuries, Carl Kaestle shows, New Yorkers created an urban school bureaucracy. Its significance lay not in the proportion of children it educated or in the social composition of the schools, which changed very little, but, rather, in the purpose and organization of schooling, which had undergone a revolution. Kaestle's book "is an attempt to explain when, why and how the schools became organized into a system." These questions are especially critical because "the central, transforming, institutional development in the history of American education was the creation of a common, uniform school system in the nineteenth century" (p. vii). Literacy and occupational training, it is important to observe, remained distinctly secondary goals in the creation of the system, whose impetus came from the desire to implant moral attitudes and American cultural traditions in the lower class of an expanding, fragmenting city.

Kaestle contrasts the relatively informal and unregulated educational arrangements of late-eighteenth-century New York with the system that emerged in the next half-century. In the earlier periods, home, church, and apprenticeship, supplemented by private but inexpensive elementary schools and a few charity schools for the poor, provided New Yorkers with a reasonably wide set of educational alternatives. The fee-charging schools themselves contained a surprisingly heterogeneous social mixture, and in the city as a whole the level of enrollment was quite high, probably rather more than half the school-age children.

In the next half-century the growth of a substantial and largely foreign lower class fostered fear, distrust, and a deliberate, escalating reliance on formal schooling to socialize the poor. The city's chief educational agency, the quasi-public, quasi-private Free (later Public) School Society, however, failed to attract either the wealthy or the very poor, and in the 1850's the proportion of children attending school remained about the same as in the 1790's, while the schools themselves had become less heterogeneous. Reformers tried a number of other expedients, but their style of "coercive institutionalization" only highlighted the incompatibility between what Kaestle calls the contraculture of street children and institutionalized reform (p. 136). Acculturation more than assimilation was the goal of schooling, whose mission was to create American habits, not to raise social status.

By the time the Public School Society turned over its schools to the new Board of Education in 1853, "schooling services in New York were consolidated, coordinated, and standardized in a process that one is tempted to call a bureaucratic revolution" (p. 159). Although the revolution happened piecemeal, without a master plan, its values represented the institutionalization of the culturally conformist mission of the schools. Nonetheless, distinctive values, efficiency and impartiality, as well as cultural standardization, underlay the adoption of systematic innovations. So thorough had the process been that, by 1853, "nearly all of the features associated with modern urban school bureaucracies were already evident" (p. 182).

According to Stanley Schultz, in an argument similar to Kaestle's, "the public school movement in the United States matured in response to what contemporaries viewed as an urban crisis," and the purpose of education became "to secure social order in a disorderly age." In their attempt to create a " 'system' in the comprehensive meaning of the word," Boston school promoters turned, Schultz argues unconvincingly, to the new factories of New England, in whose "methods of industrial organization schoolmen saw the perfect model for retooling the schools" (pp. ix–x). Thus did schools become, in Schultz's phrase, culture factories.

In Boston the Education Act of 1789 revived interest in education, which had waned during the Revolution, and established the foundation of an educational system. The Act, though creating a school committee, a Latin school, and grammar schools, left the acquisition of literacy, which was necessary for admission to these schools, to private means, either the home or the small fee-charging dame schools scattered throughout the city.

Throughout the next half-century a combination of factors —new ideas about the distinctiveness and potential of childhood, fears of family disintegration, and the loss of moral authority by the Church—turned Bostonians toward public schools as a form of social insurance "to assure stability in a time of change" (p. 68). Mounting poverty, immigration, and despair about public morality heightened the reformers' sense of urgency. Once they had considered poverty temporary; now they believed in the existence of a permanent class of the poor and a frightening, largely foreign and Catholic, culture of poverty. Although attempts to reach the children of the poor through charity schools, Sunday schools, and other means proved ineffective, they did expose the magnitude of the problem. This spurred reformers to advocate the creation of public primary schools, finally adopted in 1818 and supervised by a paternalistic though public Primary School Committee.

Schoolmen modeled their emerging systems on the "American System of Manufacturing"; they used the factory as a metaphor in their writing and attempted to centralize and standardize education in a way reminiscent of the process of production. In one sense they succeeded all too well, attracting a horde of children who overcrowded their inadequate facilities. Yet truancy and nonattendance continued to trouble school supporters, who concluded that only compulsion would bring all of the children into the schools. Proposals for compulsion generated a debate over the ownership of the child, which was eventually won by those Bostonians who believed in the right of the state to intervene between unfit parents and their children, and encouraged the state legislature to pass the first compulsory school-attendance law in the United States.

In a separate section Schultz describes the Bostonians' confrontation with the question of racial integration in the schools. The agitation of a coalition of abolitionists and blacks, who had abandoned their earlier support of segregated schools, culminated in the famous Roberts case, a temporary setback reversed a few years later in the 1850's, when the school committee ended segregation in the schools.

Striking, important parallels exist between nineteenth-century New York and Boston in the development of public education. In both cities, emphasis shifted from the education of an elite for public service to the moral education of the mass. In Colonial New York the establishment of a college preceded the founding of schools for the poor; in Boston, where a Latin school had been long established, the school committee for many years spent money more readily on grammar than on primary schools. In each place the fears and problems arising from expansion, ethnic diversification, and economic development altered the focus of education, which became the primary means of ensuring popular morality and creating cultural conformity.

In both New York and Boston as well, the early reliance on voluntarism blended into a mixture of public and private endeavor. The line between the two came to be drawn sharply in the nineteenth century by successful advocates of direct popular control. The education of the poor began in charity schools. Despite structural differences, their successors—in New York the Free (then Public) School Society and in Boston the Primary School Committee—reflected a tradition of *noblesse oblige*, relying upon a considerable amount of voluntary effort by the wealthy.

Troubled quite early by the lack of system in educational arrangements, school promoters in both cities strove to introduce coordination, standardization, and hierarchy into public education. By mid-century their efforts had matured into at least incipient bureaucracies with the rigidity and self-justifying stance that since have become their hallmark. It was in the early 1850's that a Board of Education replaced the Public School Society in New York and the Boston School Committee absorbed the Primary School Committee into a unified administrative structure, now directed by a superintendent. The process did not happen without opposition: Some came from politically and socially conservative skeptics; some from Catholics, who saw the public schools as great engines of Protestant propaganda; and some from the poor, who questioned the utility of the schools and sometimes resented their promoters. In their drive to recruit all the children, educators in both cities began at about the same time to advocate forms of compulsion or coercion, remedies logically following from their view of the social importance of schooling and the incompetence of poor parents. Advocacy of coercion, in turn, contributed to the statism inherent in educational ideology, for it enshrined in law the notion of the parental state with ultimate power over the intimate relations between parent and child.

In education-conscious Boston, according to Schultz, a little over 20 per cent of the eligible children attended school in 1789; in New York City in 1790, Kaestle estimates, the proportion was a bit over 50 per cent. It is unclear whether this is a true difference or an artifact of the methods of measurement. Should the statistics be valid, they reveal a startling and significant variation whose meaning remains to be understood.

Kaestle's view of eighteenth-century educational arrangements may be unduly optimistic, for I read his figures on school attendance as indicative of a much greater degree of class segregation in the schools than he postulates. More than that, they suggest that the children of the poor by and large were not in school. Thus it may be that the unsystematic diversity of earlier arrangements was as unsatisfactory as school reformers claimed. Nor is there evidence in his book that the variety of independent schools offered alternatives in pedagogical style or content, or that parents were aware of the range of schools in the city and chose one alternative over another in a deliberate fashion. And there is no evidence I know of to support his claim that social mobility was greater in the eighteenth than in the mid-nineteenth century. Indeed, it is equally plausible to speculate that the reverse was the case. In short, the eighteenth century appears to be a time when a stratified society neglected the poor and supported schools that served primarily the middle class.

Kaestle is not sufficiently clear about the social divisions in a nineteenth-century city and does not emphasize the great dividing line of the time—namely, the one between artisans and laborers—or the ambiguity of artisan titles, which covered everyone from journeyman to wealthy master with the same label. This problem affects his discussion of the social composition of schools, especially of the Free Academy, which, on the basis of the evidence he presents, was an institution that in no way met the democratic objectives of its sponsors, as he argues.

Despite the title of his book, the story Kaestle tells does not describe an evolution as much as a shift from one set of educational arrangements to a distinctly different variety. And this, especially, is why it supports my argument in Chapter

l about competing models of organization. In fact, he may
have emphasized unduly the continuity between the Public
School Society and its successor, the Board of Education. The
rhetoric of the different sides in the controversy that led to
the Society's demise should be taken seriously, for the voluntarist, paternalist ethos at the core of the Society differed fundamentally from the idea of popular control underlying the
Board of Education. Thus it is more precise to view the development Kaestle describes as a nonevolutionary change of
direction from a stage of diversity to one of voluntarism to another of public bureaucracy, with the boundaries between
stages blurred.

Schultz's book, neither clearly focused nor tightly organized, sometimes appears rambling and repetitious. Unlike
Kaestle's, it ends abruptly with no conclusion or recapitula-
tion. There are some serious difficulties in the argument as
well. First, although Schultz contends that educators consciously modeled the schools on recently developed methods
of factory production, he gives no evidence that any educator
actually copied factory techniques. The use of the factory as a
metaphor hardly shows deliberate modeling, for metaphors
have various uses, including, as has frequently been the case
in American education, the appropriation to the schools of
the prestige of other social institutions. Nor is there evidence
in the book permitting detailed comparison of the internal
administrations of factories and schools. Similarities may have
been superficial, more than likely, as I suggested in Chapter 2,
reflecting the response of men with similar sets of values and
priorities to problems of scale, diversity, and complexity—by
fostering the division of labor and greater centralization.

Interestingly, in 1806 De Witt Clinton made the first reference I have found to the school as a factory, a reference
quoted by Schultz toward the end of his book. Clinton was
praising the factory-like qualities of the monitorial system,
speaking about fifteen years *before* the development of the

"American System of Manufacturing." In fact, had school promoters wanted to copy the factory, they would probably have adhered longer to the monitorial system, which tried to routinize schooling more than any other procedure before or since. However, its rigid qualities appalled nineteenth-century educational reformers, who argued for a distinct softening of pedagogy and motivational technique in ways not at all compatible with a factory model. Schultz nevertheless ignores the prominent stream of early- and mid-nineteenth-century educational writing dealing with the content and method of education as distinct from its external organization. Finally, in their campaigns to promote public education, schoolmen, as I observed in Chapter 1, acted more like evangelical ministers than factory managers, and in their writings references to the teacher as minister are, I suspect, more frequent than references to the factory.

Schultz's emphasis on bureaucracy as an early organizing force obscures the variation between stages in the development of public education. Surely it is an exaggeration to see Bostonians striving continuously since the 1630's to create an educational system. And the Act of 1789, though it created a school committee, can hardly be considered the foundation of a contemporary educational system, since it required literacy for entrance to the schools, made no provision for the education of the poor, and in other ways revealed the blurred boundary between public and private still prevalent at the time. On a different issue, it was not really contradictory, as Schultz claims, for schoolmen to try to bring all of the children into school, even though those who were there already overtaxed the facilities. If the actual role of the school was primarily custodial, it could accomplish its purpose even if children were herded into poorly ventilated rooms in which education in any meaningful sense was impossible. Nor would it be unreasonable for the schoolmen to hope that they could increase public appreciation and hence expenditure by demonstrating that they served all the children.

Nineteenth-century schooling, it should be stressed, had at least two social functions that neither Kaestle nor Schultz describes. One was disciplining the work force, as in early industrial England. This meant teaching an essentially rural and nonindustrial population the norms of modern urban life through fostering a sense of the importance of time, rewarding achieved rather than ascribed qualities, and, over all, substituting an inner-direction appropriate to an anonymous city for the more visible authority of tradition and community in simpler places. The other social role was responding to middle-class anxieties and aspirations. A heightened concern with adolescence and a perception that formal schooling was replacing occupational inheritance as a means for maintaining status across generations impelled people of middling wealth to encourage the expansion and improvement of educational facilities. Although promoters spoke of its benefits to the poor, the new school system best served the moderately affluent.

III

When did urban educational systems originate? Schultz's answer, I have observed, is far too early. On the other hand, as Carl Kaestle has noted, Marvin Lazerson, in *Origins of the Urban School*, does not reach quite far enough into the past. Lazerson, observes Kaestle, uses studies of the introduction of the kindergarten, manual training, and civic instruction in ten Massachusetts cities to demonstrate that in the late nineteenth and early twentieth centuries "school reformers moved from an attempt to reform the society through the schools to an attempt to fit the school child for his place in society, and, most important, that in the process the school moved from a common curriculum to a differentiated curric-

ulum, a momentous and seemingly irreversible linear development in the history of American education. Thus the water-
shed is divided into two sub-periods: the first, roughly to
1900, when reformers tried to change social attitudes and
conditions, and the second, 1900–1915, when they turned to
adjusting the child to the existing system."

The anxieties that underlay the campaign for social reform
through schooling had a history which Lazerson understates.
As we have observed, a sense of urban crisis, a fear of the
alien, and a firm belief in the moral inadequacy of the poor
family all formed part of the vision of the generation of social policy-makers who, roughly a half-century before the
period Lazerson writes about, had created the first systems of
public education. The cycle of reform zeal that ended, para-
doxically, in the creation of bureaucracy had waned by late
in the nineteenth century, and the developments Lazerson
describes represent its reawakening, another upswing in the
periodic cycle of social reform in American society. However, this is a small problem in an excellent book, which is
thoroughly researched, cogently argued, clearly organized and
written—in short, a major contribution to the history of
American education.

Rather than concentrate on the question of precedents, it
is more useful to focus on two important issues raised by
Lazerson's book. One of these is interpretive: the extent to
which the character of American education changed during
the late nineteenth and early twentieth centuries. The other
is more methodological: the implications of the choice between theme and process as the organizing principle of historical study.

The character of American education, according to Lazerson, changed fundamentally in this period in response to
two developments. First, educators abandoned their rural
idealism and ambivalence toward industrialization. Second, at

the same time they introduced curricula differentiated by the occupational destination of students. This innovation rested on a redefinition of democracy in education, which no longer meant the promotion of social harmony through the intermingling of all students in a common educational experience. Rather, it now signified the provision of specific skills that would enable each group of students to leave school properly prepared for its occupational future.

Lazerson makes a convincing case for the institutionalization of the new notion of democracy through the differentiated curricula sponsored by the vocational-education movement. Thus, the issue is not the existence of these developments but their significance. Did they represent a break with the principles upon which urban school systems had originally been erected earlier in the nineteenth century? Or can their introduction be reconciled with my interpretation, put forth earlier in this book, that the fundamental structure of American urban education had been set by about 1880? The extent of structural change in urban education remains a more important issue than the disappearance of rural idealism, a development that Lazerson establishes much less convincingly. Instances of ambivalence toward industry and rural idealism abound in twentieth-century educational literature and in school texts. And it is doubtful that schoolmen ever have been free of the uneasiness about urban and industrial life that has permeated American culture.

Nonetheless, the ideal of a unitary, undifferentiated high school curriculum, defended as late as the 1890's by the Committee of Ten, gave way within a few decades to the division of students into tracks based upon an expected future, predicted by their academic performance as young children and the social class of their parents. Though momentous, the division of high schools into college and noncollege tracks and the establishment of vocational and commercial high schools represented extensions of the principles upon which educational systems had been founded, and they did not upset the already existing bureaucratic structure of urban education.

As I have argued in Chapter 2, by late in the nineteenth century many urban school systems had *already* become fully developed bureaucratic organizations, and the introduction of vocational education did not reverse or substantially alter that development. Indeed, it even could be argued that bureaucratic structure proved more powerful than the original concept of vocational education, which had to be reshaped before it could be incorporated permanently as a feature of American urban education. For Lazerson points to the fascinating and unsuccessful attempt in Massachusetts to institutionalize a system of vocational education distinct from the public schools and linked closely with industry. By the time that effort began in the early twentieth century, however, professional educators had formed an interest group strong enough to resist the effective implementation of a rival organization, and in a relatively short time the public schoolmen won control of vocational education, which they incorporated in an altered fashion into their system.

In fact, vocational education fitted well within existing educational systems. For it represented the extension of the social role and structural principles of urban school systems to an altered demographic situation. Despite the common-school ideology, urban education always had been differentiated. Among young students, residential segregation managed to keep intact a fair amount of social-class division within urban schools. Until well into the twentieth century, moreover, most students left school quite early, around the age of thirteen or fourteen, and only a small minority went on to high school. Within the high school no need for a differentiated curriculum existed, because the relatively few students who attended generally sought the same sort of education as preparation for university entrance, for teaching, or for commercial careers. Early in the twentieth century, for reasons that have not been explored adequately, young people began to stay in school for longer periods, and it soon became apparent to schoolmen that they had a new clientele within the high schools: children of immigrant and working-class parents, for whom the old curriculum appeared manifestly inadequate. Vocational education appeared to be an appropriate and egalitarian response to the entrance of large numbers of children who would work with their hands when they left high school. In fact, though, the introduction of vocational education allowed school systems to continue to offer their traditional advantages to the middle classes; through vocational education school systems formalized their long-standing participation in the reproduction rather than the alteration of class structure.

Thus, in the largest sense, vocational education permitted school systems to retain their traditional social function; at the same time it reflected the organizational principles upon which educational bureaucracies had been erected. Schoolmen long had stressed the importance of exact classification to the development of educational systems. Specialization and the division of labor, they argued, were the fundamental principles of modern organizational development, and upon them schoolmen spun out their plans for elaborate educational systems. At first their goal was simply the introduction of age-grading into schools; then it became the creation of a hierarchy of schools within each system; afterward, as Lazerson shows, it became the introduction of differentiated educational programs. From this perspective, vocational education represented an elaboration of the bureaucratic impulse that had been at work in urban social organization since the middle decades of the nineteenth century.

The second issue I shall discuss here concerns not the substance of Lazerson's argument but the thematic way in which he chose to organize his book and the consequences of that decision. Although he studied closely the history of education in ten cities (which, incidentally, is exactly the kind of re-search that is desperately required if we are to gain some con-crete idea of what actually happened in American education), Lazerson does not offer extended case histories that show how given cities wrestled with their educational problems over time. Rather, each chapter shows what people in many places thought and did about a particular issue: the kindergarten, manual training, vocational education, evening classes, in-struction in civics. Nonetheless, a number of common themes unify the separate discussions: the social problems schoolmen faced; their attitudes toward industrialization, immigrants, and cities; the role of private philanthropy in stimulating in-novation; and the half-hearted way in which school systems actually incorporated many reforms.

Though Lazerson's thematic organization has distinct ad-vantages, it nonetheless slights process: From his book we are quite clear about the differences in ideas and practices be-tween two points in time but not at all sure about the pro-cess through which change took place. We are convinced, to take one example, that the goal of manual education shifted from the teaching of underlying principles to training for specific trades. But we are not given a precise explanation about why that shift took place, how it found expression within individual school systems, or who its sponsors and op-ponents were. We learn that virtually every innovation met resistance: In a number of places not very many children went to kindergarten; manual training was undercut by its subordinate, even trivial, place in the curriculum. Yet both of these had been highly praised and well publicized. What, ex-actly, went wrong? Lazerson does not provide a very detailed or satisfying answer. And the reason lies partly within the method he has chosen to organize his book.

Educational innovations take place in particular contexts. Social structure, political divisions, the nature of the educa-tional system, the demography of particular cities—all of these interacted in a complex way in decisions about kindergartens, manual training, or evening schools. With remarkable skill Lazerson has shown the striking similarity in the patterns and outcomes of educational change in a variety of places, and his book provides evidence of the common elements in the educational response within Massachusetts cities. However, only detailed study of individual cases will reveal the dynamics of the general pattern. To answer the questions about process that this book leaves dangling, Lazerson's material should be disaggregated and rearranged into a series of case studies of individual cities which attempt to assess the relationship among society, demography, politics, and educational change. In addition to a thematic portrait, that is, we need a careful dissection of the forces at work in individual cities as people sought to introduce *simultaneously* kindergartens, vocational training, evening classes, and new forms of civic education.

The analysis of educational reform requires not only a detailed examination of case histories but an imaginative and broad conception of historical data. It calls for an attempt to assess the claims of schoolmen, reformers, and politicians against social reality. To take one important example: Schoolpeople and reformers consistently criticized the family life of immigrants and of the urban poor. The assumed inability of the poor to raise their children properly, in fact, underlay the kindergarten movement; and the instability, immorality, and brutality of the poor family became very nearly axiomatic in nineteenth-century reform thought. But was the prevailing image of the poor family accurate? Perhaps reformers confused cultural difference with inadequacy and immorality; perhaps they misread the effects of poverty and industrial exploitation as disorganization and instability; perhaps early kindergartens did not successfully attract the children of the poor because their families knew very well the assumptions of the founders. None of this is certain, though all of it is plausible, and issues such as these must be confronted if history is to move beyond the ideology of reform and the institutional record of success and failure to an explanation of innovation that takes into account an accurate conception of its social context.

Marvin Lazerson concentrates on the introduction of new educational programs, new forms of schooling, and a new ideology of educational purpose. But he virtually neglects another important theme in urban education during the same period: the controversy over its control and administration. David Tyack, in contrast, devotes most of *The One Best System* to an examination of the transformation of haphazard collections of village schools into urban systems. Although in his last chapter Tyack does discuss vocational education and the kindergarten, he concentrates on the development of organization: the origin of bureaucratic features, professionalization, and the contest over control. Read together, Lazerson's and Tyack's books provide a remarkably full account of what happened in urban education during the late nineteenth and early twentieth centuries.

Although Tyack offers an overview of developments from early in the nineteenth century to 1973, he focuses most sharply on the years from, roughly, 1870 to 1920. His book, unlike Lazerson's, is not a monograph but, rather, a broad and successful synthesis combining monographic studies of the last several years (including his own) with the rich but largely unanalyzed material gathered by schoolpeople and social scientists early in the century. Lively, full of detail, and gracefully written, Tyack's book will serve nicely as a text, an introduction to recent educational historiography, or a reliable and readable account of the origins of urban educational systems.

In Tyack's view early-nineteenth-century educational arrangements in both countryside and town remained unsystematic and relatively informal. The community was the school, and the school was the community. Under the pressures of urban life this informality gave way to a sustained effort to systematize and rationalize schooling; through a somewhat haphazard process bureaucracy emerged as the organizing principle of urban education. Educators sponsored this process, which offered them career-lines within education and the opportunity to exercise power over large organizations. However, Tyack notes, opportunities were reserved largely for men, who ran the new educational systems, staffed largely by corps of subordinate women. (Tyack does not point out, however, the extent to which teaching provided a new vocational opportunity for women at a time when most of them could find work only as domestic servants or seamstresses, or, later, in factories. Despite their subordinate position, teaching must have appeared to many young women a very desirable alternative to a life spent idly at home or in domestic drudgery.)

Although schoolmen developed an increasingly articulate and coherent case for the importance of professional management, the division of labor, and specialization, their efforts to construct powerful bureaucratic empires did not lack opposition. This opposition, Tyack points out, arose from cultural rather than class conflicts. The late-nineteenth-century intellectual critics of school bureaucracy did not have the impact that spokesmen for cultural issues exercised: In some places religion, in others language, became a controversial question, often entangled with conflicts between Democrats and Republicans. Ethnic spokesmen often perceived quite accurately that centralization represented an attempt to standardize the people by wiping out cultural distinctions. Aggressive Protestantism, temperance, and English-language chauvinism added up to the same score: an attempt to assimilate newcomers to a predefined American standard.

The men and women Tyack calls "administrative progressives" also attacked what they called bureaucracy. These elite municipal reformers sought to centralize school systems as part of a more general attempt to reassume control of urban public administration. By bureaucracy, however, they meant red tape and clumsy administration, not a hierarchical, professionally administered, rule-governed form of organization. Indeed, their attempt to fashion educational administration on a corporate model with a small board of directors guided by a powerful executive officer represented an attempt to further professionalize the school systems that existed. The "administrative progressives," as Tyack writes, tried to introduce a new and more streamlined type of bureaucracy.

Tyack's detailed summaries of the process of centralization within a number of cities confirm the argument offered in Chapter 3 of this book: namely, that a class-based, essentially conservative municipal reform movement formed one important strand in educational "progressivism." Tyack shows that in every city where the process has been studied, a social elite attempted to wrest control of the schools by replacing the large, ward-based school committees with small boards elected from the city at large. In every case reformers presented their program as an attempt to lift education out of the corruption of politics and to introduce more efficient and professional management. In reality these programs represented campaigns to shift political power within cities from one group to another.

Though the administrative progressives usually succeeded, Tyack notes, their newly centralized school boards never had the effects their sponsors predicted. Municipal reformers quite naïvely overestimated the impact of administrative change on the operation of fully developed bureaucracies. Smart mayors, political bosses, and superintendents manipulated the new school boards quite as effectively as the old. Indeed, the most vivid lesson to emerge from administrative progressivism at the turn of the century was negative. Changing the size of a school board or the method by which it is elected does little to redistribute power within the system or to alter the experience of the children who pass through it.

Of course, the managers of educational systems, Tyack points out, looked with pride at their accomplishments in the early twentieth century: Increasing numbers of children attended school for longer periods of time; there were new forms and levels of schooling; and education became, for them at least, more "scientific." Nonetheless, from the viewpoint of their clients, urban education did not become more satisfactory. Indeed, school systems continued to have the same victims.

Schoolpeople adopted social control and social efficiency as overriding objectives in the late nineteenth and early twentieth centuries, and these goals conflicted with the libertarian rhetoric of reform theory during the same period. Although schoolpeople sometimes adopted the recommendations of educational reformers such as John Dewey, they bent those innovations to fit rather than shake the existing systems.

However, no ambivalence restrained the warmth with which schoolpeople embraced testing. They needed a technology to differentiate children easily and defensibly into the various aspects of the diversifying educational systems. The development of IQ tests during World War I represented an innovation on which schoolmen seized with predictable and uncritical eagerness. Science enabled schoolpeople to label groups of children inferior; often those groupings reflected ethnic origin or race. Testing legitimized segregation within American education.

Throughout this period, superintendents, professors of education, and other administrators sponsored most educational change. Teachers, Tyack observes, played a very passive role, and for good reason. Generally without tenure, subject to annual reappointment, paid miserably, teachers lived with insecurity, though for a brief time it appeared that the militancy of Margaret Haley might galvanize women teachers into an effective and united force.

In short, Tyack argues that American education has always had its victims: the poor, blacks, and, it must be remembered, the teachers. Their plight has not been accidental but, rather, is the unintended consequence of a system erected carefully and painstakingly. Victimization has been the predictable and inevitable consequence of the American system of education.

Though he criticizes the consequences of educational history, Tyack retreats before the uncomfortable and radical conclusions to which his evidence quite clearly appears to point. Tyack presents a damning case against the educational system but concludes, with less evidence than I, at any rate, need, that often it did open alternatives for many students. In fact, his entire discussion of the social function of public education remains unclear. Tyack appears to avoid the logic of his historical account that school systems have institutionalized and perpetuated the prejudices and inequities of American society. Thus he backs away from the question of motives. Early in the book he argues that victimization in American education has been systematic; however, throughout the remaining chapters he maintains in a number of places that it would be incorrect to impute malign purposes to the architects of unequal school systems or to the people who injected their racism into the origins of the testing movement. Tyack, of course, has met the dilemma that I already discussed briefly: If these were all decent, honorable people, how could they deliberately have done anything morally reprehensible? On the other hand, though, we might just as well ask: Can a publicly sustained and universal system that has steadily victimized its most helpless members for a century be simply the product of lack of foresight?

Tyack, probably unwillingly, gives history an aura of inevitability in his analysis. In the circumstances, how could men have acted otherwise? The alternatives he presents do not appear, in retrospect, to have been as persuasive or practical as people of the time often thought them to be. Did people of that era, then, have less choice than we do today? Or is the reform movement of the present willfully ignoring the reality, which dictates an inevitable, if unfortunate, course of action? If we do not believe there is only one choice today, can we accept the implication that, historically, only one existed? Though Tyack would disagree with this reading of the evidence he presents, that is a dilemma with which his book leaves me. However, it may be more helpful, as I shall elaborate later, to view action as nearly always consistent with self-interest. People of an earlier period may not have been malicious, but they did act on motives rooted, perhaps not even consciously, in their social-class interests. They succeeded, very simply, because they had the power that other groups lacked. Those class interests, as is demonstrated by the similar educational histories of other countries with different political systems, were not solely the interests of a capitalist class but, more properly, were those of the sponsors, managers, and principal beneficiaries of the emerging technocratic and institutional state that has come to dominate our lives in the twentieth century.

The definition and role of social class form another of the complex issues with which Tyack does not quite come to grips. Although at one point he asserts that ethnic and religious differences cross-cut class distinctions, his treatment of class and ethnicity misses the subtle interplay between the two forces in American history. Certainly, they are not identical, but when ethnicity and economic position coincide, it becomes extremely difficult to say that one rather than the other formed the operative force at any given moment. And this coincidence has happened often, as in the case of the Irish in the mid-nineteenth century, the Italians late in the century, or the blacks throughout most of American history. A coherent argument in favor of either class or ethnicity must be based on a theory about their operation and influence, an issue which Tyack does not consider.

Finally, relations among class, ethnicity, and culture, must in part be investigated empirically. Like Lazerson, Tyack sometimes accepts a little too readily the view of social reality offered by schoolpeople and reformers. Nineteenth-century communities, we now know from studies of geographic mobility, lacked the integration with which nostalgia has invested them. They could not have been isolated islands, and even rural schools could not have had quite the integral relation with their clientele that Tyack assumes. Similarly, we must be very careful, as I have said before, about accepting without qualification the view of lower-class and immigrant family life that social critics are still so fond of offering. In some areas there is no substitute for the facts, and when a different sort of research discovers just what they are, nineteenth-century urban life may appear substantially different from what we have long believed.

IV

Neither Lazerson nor Tyack attempts to plot the interconnections between educational thought and contemporary intellectual history. Although they show quite clearly that educational reform around the turn of the century reflected the pervasive search for order and prevailing spirit of municipal reform, they do not explore its relationship to the intellectual foundations of the corporate state or to the broader pattern of American liberalism. That exploration, fortunately, has been undertaken by other scholars, most notably by Clarence Karier and his colleagues in *Roots of Crisis*. Confronting boldly the uneasy questions that Tyack avoids, their book offers a stunning and radical indictment of American educational reform theory and practice in the twentieth century.

In the intellectual history of the last decade no trend is more prominent than the repudiation of liberalism. Not long ago considered the culmination of Western political tradition, liberalism—characterized by a pragmatic temper, a faith in rationality and science, and a dedication to melioristic social reform—has been rejected by both the political right and the left. To the left, it came to symbolize a naïve faith that the world was getting better, masking the fact that most major social problems were worsening at home and that liberal Americans were practicing genocide in Asia. Liberalism became the rationalization offered by a smug middle class to ensure that social change did not dismember fundamental, unequal social and economic structures.

In the attack on liberalism, historians have played a major role by re-evaluating its most cherished achievements and its heroes, especially the movement for political and social reform generally called progressivism, which gathered steam in the late nineteenth century. Most of us have been nurtured on the belief that progressivism represented a quickening of the forces of democracy and benevolence in American life through an attempt to cleanse government of corruption; to attack problems of poverty, disease, and distress; and to formulate a theory of positive and humane state action. It has been the task of younger and politically radical historians to challenge this interpretation, often with devastating effectiveness, by showing that at the heart of what we have called progressivism were racism, a yearning for social control, and a desire to make the world safe for the corporation.

The historiography of education usually reflects broader currents in American thought and scholarship, and progressive education often has been portrayed as introducing a series of liberating changes in American educational thought and practice. The ideas of Dewey, the activities of Jane Addams, and the work of curriculum reformers have been interpreted as attempts to democratize the educational system by bending it to the needs of a poor and immigrant population, making schooling appropriate for the city child, injecting warmth and humanity into the classroom, extending the range of social services performed by public institutions, and, in sum, turning the school into a positive force for social reform. The most persuasive and explicit statement of the relation between progressive education, viewed in this fashion, and progressivism in politics is offered in Lawrence Cremin's study *The Transformation of the School*. There he defines progressive education as "the educational phase of American Progressivism writ large."

Despite the changing evaluation of the progressive tradition in American life, Cremin's book will remain a classic. Its succinct summations of ideas, woven into a coherent narrative describing the intellectual movement, will be of enduring value even though the interpretive framework in which the book is set will be sharply questioned. This is because Cremin connects progressivism in education with the older and more traditional view of progressivism in American life.

But what if one takes a different view of America and its past? What if we believe that the educational innovations and ideas usually labeled progressive in fact have reflected a broader social movement toward order and control? This is what revisionist historians find in the history of the twentieth century, and *Roots of Crisis* begins to spell out the implications of this social critique for a critique of the schools.

In the introduction the authors state that their assumptions about America and its past differ sharply from those of the men they label "liberal historians," notably Richard Hofstadter, Merle Curti, Henry Steele Commager, and Lawrence Cremin. To the authors of *Roots of Crisis*,

. . . if one views the present world more critically, liberal history will be found short on meaningful criticism and long on apology. . . . If one starts with the assumption that this society is in fact racist, fundamentally materialistic, and institutionally structured to protect vested interests, the past takes on vastly different meanings [p. 5].

Their book is an attempt to show how those meanings may be used to explain the history of American education in the twentieth century.

The book remains in essence a collection of essays, several published elsewhere, which share a common point of view but are diverse in other respects. The topics reflect the interests of the individual authors rather than offering any systematic account of the development of education, and there is a good deal of overlap between some of them. The diversity of the essays, in quality as well as subject matter, makes it difficult to discuss them collectively. Consequently, here I will comment separately on some of the contributions of each author.

Paul Violas has three pieces, of which the most provocative is an essay on Jane Addams. His view of Addams's motivation sees within her humanitarian concern a desire for social control. "At the heart of her effort was an attempt to replace the social control implicit in the village community with controls more suitable to an urban environment" (p. 70). His essay is useful because it raises the issue of whether there was another side of Jane Addams and, by implication, another side of the settlement movement she represented. It is undeniable that an emphasis on control and collective effort formed a key strand in her notion of democracy and in the policies she advocated. Nonetheless, Violas's interpretation is somewhat one-sided because it neglects the emphasis on process that also was a part of her definition of democracy. Her famous phrase, that a good is not worth having unless all men participate in its attainment, was not merely, as he suggests, an effort to enlist the energies of all in the attainment of goals formulated by an elite. The context in which she made the observation—a comment on the dissatisfactions that arose from living in even the best of company towns—shows Jane Addams's remarkable insight into the relationships between social process and social goals. This understanding did not find its way into public policy for more than a half-century, when it became the only revolutionary and least honored part of the late and unsuccessful War on Poverty.

Violas also suggests that her insistence on the importance of popularizing ideas indicates she believed in the legitimacy and necessity of propaganda. But his quotations from her writings do not show anything of the sort. Rather, they reflect a serious attempt by Jane Addams to grapple with the still unsolved problem of how to promote a mass understanding of complex and unconventional ideas. In the same way, it is somewhat far-fetched to view as repressive her insistence on the importance of humanizing the industrial process by teaching workers about the history, nature, and significance of their industries. Perhaps accommodation to oppressive working conditions would have been an unintended outcome if her ideas had ever succeeded. But she was responding to the very real problem of worker alienation. A recurring hope of intellectuals has been that the divorce between life and work, one of the most unfortunate consequences of modernization in Western countries, can be overcome. Even now, many men and women must work long hours at boring and routine jobs. At a time when manpower requirements were even higher than they are today, the good of everyone depended on those jobs being done. Proposals such as those made by Jane Addams admittedly were utopian; in terms of the sociology of work and the psychology of workers there is no way they could succeed. But they were not part of a repressive philosophy.

The issue Addams was addressing continues to confront

policy-makers. One has only to read the statements about the work ethic that disfigured recent national political campaigns in both Canada and the United States to realize that the definition and valuation of work have become controversial. If worker alienation is a problem, can it be solved by trying to connect workers with industry through education, or by offering them a share in the decision-making? Or are these pipe dreams? Can the problem be solved better by introducing enough technological innovations to reduce the work week to an absolute minimum, while at the same time providing facilities for increased leisure activity? We are wrestling with the same problem Jane Addams did, but we are a little more cynical and a lot less utopian.

In the same way we must be careful about the meaning we attribute to the collectivist emphasis—the frequent anti-individualistic bias—that appears in the writings of some progressive theorists. We must be careful not to dismiss this solely as an effort to make the world comfortable for corporate capitalism. It is just as congruent with socialism, maybe even more so. Indeed, there seems to be little inherent connection between individualism and freedom, on the one hand, and either socialism or capitalism.

Interestingly, if one takes as correct Philip Slater's radical critique of American society,* then rampant individualism is at the core of our sickness. Worship of unbridled liberty and undisturbed privacy, he argues, have become pathological symptoms of contemporary culture. Perhaps Jane Addams and John Dewey saw the same problem Slater does: a nation of people hell-bent on their personal satisfaction at the expense of anyone else's. American individualism may have created the very situation that radical critics of progressive collectivism feared. There is much irony here, and a dilemma of great complexity and significance.

There is a final point which Violas's article and others in

* Philip Slater, *The Pursuit of Loneliness* (New York: Knopf, 1961).

the book raise indirectly, a point I have discussed earlier as well—namely, the difficulties revisionist historians have in coming to terms with benevolence. In an earlier period historians could accept benevolence as the expression of deeply felt ideals, often stemming from religious belief. Now that is less easy. On the one hand, the social-class origins of philanthropists are only too apparent, and our awareness of how people subconsciously act out their guilt or rationalize their actions makes it difficult to accept motivations at face value. On the other hand, interpretations that acknowledge only motives of social control or reduce all benevolent activity to neurosis remain unsatisfactory. They accord poorly with common sense and everyday experience. What revisionist historians lack (and, as I have said, I certainly include myself among the inadequate here) is an understanding of how activity is integrated with the psychology of the individual and the sociology of ideas in his time.

Some of the same themes exist in the work of Joel Spring. In his essay "Education as a Form of Social Control," Spring distinguishes two aspects of social control in education: "maintaining social order" and "differentiating pupils" by their social origins and occupational destinations. These he considers the primary functions schools have served in the twentieth century, when they "became *the* agency charged with the responsibility of maintaining social order and cohesion and of instilling individuals with codes of conduct and social values that would insure the stability of existing social relationships" (p. 30).

Spring argues his case primarily by examining the writing of sociologists such as Edward A. Ross and by discussing the early testing movement. In a brief article it is difficult for him to establish the case conclusively, and it is perhaps better to reserve judgment about the adequacy of his argument. One assumption, though, bears scrutiny, namely his assertion that "by the beginning of the twentieth century, industrialization and urbanization had severely eroded the influence of family, church, and community on individual behavior" (p. 30). By accepting this account, Spring accepts the same premises on which Ross and other sociologists—whom he criticizes—based their cases. There is mounting evidence, however, that these premises were wrong. The family probably survived social upheaval with a good deal more resiliency than has usually been imagined. The lives of the poor and the immigrant very likely were much more organized and regular than nativists would have liked others to believe. And the nineteenth-century village also lacked the tranquil stability that nostalgic intellectuals imputed to it. In short, in order to understand the social history of the twentieth century one must begin by questioning the basic perceptions of the people who then were formulating social policy. It is wrong to argue with them on their own terms. The quarrel, as I have said before, should begin with their premises.

Interesting, too, is Spring's attempt to argue that youth culture is an effective source of social change. His thesis that youth has switched from an age category to a cultural phenomenon is probably a sound and important insight, though his prediction of a permanent countercultural movenemt may be unwarranted. The ability of corporate capitalism to co-opt and castrate the youth culture, as the recent history of the clothing and entertainment industries show, is one of the more depressing, though predictable, phenomena of recent years. In this process establishment forces have received powerful indirect assistance from the economic recession and resulting job shortages. But if a true counterculture is possible only in a time of affluence, this raises a lot of questions about just how "counter" it really is.

In his essay "Education and the Cold War: The Role of James B. Conant," Thomas Grissom extends the argument of the book from the relations of education and corporate capitalism to the role of education in the development of national and foreign policy. In this tough-minded, sophisticated analysis, Grissom advances the important argument that

> . . . those educational "events" designated as Cold War spin-offs . . . were less the result of diplomatic machinations after Yalta or a fear of communists at home and abroad than they were the natural extension of a broadly conceived and widely accepted view of the role of education in a modern industrialized nation state. [p. 178]

Grissom convincingly argues his case through an analysis of the work and influence of James B. Conant, whose intellect and writing he appreciates as well as criticizes. He penetrates to the assumptions and weaknesses at the root of Conant's work, particularly the avoidance of issues of wealth and power and the tendency to identify national welfare with the preservation of the nation state.

I have saved for last a discussion of the bold and important essays by Clarence Karier, certainly the most impressive in the book. Their boldness lies in their reach, for each covers a large segment of history, attempting to integrate the development of schooling with an array of social and economic forces.

In "Business Values and the Education State," Karier argues that "the educational state that emerged in twentieth-century America did so ultimately as an instrument of those economic and political elites who managed the American corporate state" (p. 6). Historically, schools have taught "the norms necessary to adjust the young to the changing patterns of the economic system as well as to the society's more permanent values" (p. 7). More specifically, they have performed three functions—training, testing and sorting, and holding—altering their emphasis with changing manpower needs. Karier's case is difficult to prove conclusively in one brief essay, for it spans American history. But as the first essay in the book, it raises critical questions and sets the stage appropriately for the chapters that follow.

Karier's second essay, "Liberalism and the Quest for Orderly Change," directly confronts the weaknesses of American liberalism. His well-argued contention is that, whenever liberals have been forced to take sides, they have moved to the right. Given their history, he can see no reason why they should behave any differently in confrontations to come. For Karier, the shifts to the right have been not accidental results of temperament but the product of tendencies deeply embedded within liberal political thought. As a way of examining these tendencies, he analyzes themes in the work of John Dewey, who stands in the essay as a kind of Everyman, exemplifying the strengths and weaknesses of liberal thought and action. The strength of Karier's position lies in his ability to connect twentieth-century liberalism with a long intellectual tradition, one that might be called the Enlightenment notion of progress, a long-standing faith that the expert application of science can solve all material, social, and human problems. Its heritage, which lives within most of us, is an over-optimistic reliance on science, technological solutions, and experts. An obsession with efficiency, concern for social engineering, deference to technical expertise—and the concomitant denigration of philosophical and moral considerations—are the most prominent features of the tradition Karier probes. As a consequence:

> Neither science nor technology was effectively employed to enhance democracy (rule by the people). Rather, science and technology became effective tools with which the powerful controlled the social system. Perhaps the liberal faith in science and technology is not an adequate substitute for a philosophy of man [pp. 106–7].

In "Testing for Order and Control in the Corporate Liberal

State," Karier shows how faith in science coalesced with the educational goals of the corporate state. For many people this essay will be the highlight of the book. It should be read by everyone concerned with education. In a persuasive examination of the origins of psychological testing, Karier reveals how foundations actively promoted the development of testing. At the same time he makes it undeniably clear that the values and attitudes of psychologists who developed IQ tests, often also leaders of the eugenics movement, were racist and elitist. These psychologists incorporated their social and moral biases into their theories and tests, creating a sophisticated rationale for the construction of a meritocracy in which social mobility has been strictly regulated. Early intelligence tests, Karier demonstrates, reflected the social-class order because they were based on it. The results of the tests were a familiar and self-fulfilling prophecy.

Early testers propagated the idea that measured intelligence and moral worth were closely connected, thus helping to legitimize social inequality. On the basis of scientific evidence the poor were both unintelligent and unworthy. In a similar way, testing has reinforced power and privilege, Karier shows, by cloaking the transfer of status and affluence from one generation to the next in the guise of a meritocracy in which talent finds its reward.

Some readers of this essay have criticized Karier for espousing a conspiracy theory of history. He does not. There was no conspiracy to grind the poor and perpetuate the privilege of the rich. Foundations supported projects that they thought were in the general interest of American society; psychologists believed in the general social value of their own activity.

Nonetheless, ideas cannot be divorced from social structure, and definitions of the general good differ according to their source. It is an elementary point in the sociology of knowledge—not surprising or shocking or nasty—that people with wealth and power in America have acted in ways that have served themselves best, and on balance their social theories support those actions. Karier has shown that testing as a concept, a practice, and a movement has its origins in social structure as well as science. The moral is that testing cannot be reformed.

Few people will react neutrally to *Roots of Crisis*. It is an angry book that challenges the intellectual, political, and professional heritage of many of the people who should read it. In its best passages it manages to question what we are doing as educators, and even as human beings. Given what we know about schooling today, there are very good grounds for supposing that the historical vision of the authors is generally correct. In any event, the burden of proof no longer lies with those who argue that education is and has been unequal. It lies, rather, with those who would defend the system.

V

Given the history Karier describes, we should expect liberalism to co-opt and tame the contemporary movement for radical school reform. There are in fact plenty of indications that this is precisely what is happening. No one exemplifies the process more clearly than Charles Silberman, whose recent and widely publicized book *Crisis in the Classroom* is a strangely comforting indictment of American education. The cause of the "crisis in the classroom," he would have us believe, is a simple failure to think clearly and honestly. Consequently, remedies for the schools' problems do not require the replacement of present social or educational structures; they demand, rather, the introduction of sensible and humane reforms into institutions that now exist. Mr. Silberman, in fact, has little use for most educational radicals, and his book will stand as a classic example of the liberal reform approach to American education in the late twentieth century. Therein lie its strengths and weaknesses. As a catalog of educational horrors and a dissection of the weaknesses of several reform theories and practices, Crisis in the Classroom, though not original, is intelligent, clear, and compelling. As an analysis of the causes of educational failure, it is shallow and even evasive. Finally, as a program for change, Crisis in the Classroom is inadequate and, worse, misleading.

The length of the book, its wealth of detail, its professional presentation, its sponsorship, its publicity—all these factors lend it an air of authenticity and, almost, legitimacy. There is no doubt that it will be as widely read, widely considered, and influential as a book about education can be. For that reason, it is all the more important to explore with some care its adequacy as a diagnosis and proposed treatment for American education.

Let us consider Silberman's indictment of American education: first, that the schools fail, and indeed have always failed, to act as equalizers of opportunity. The rhetoric of social mobility notwithstanding, schools have done remarkably little to counteract racial, social, and economic inequities within American society.

More than that, Silberman indicts the schools for their repressive and spirit-breaking quality. Preoccupied with order and control, schools, he observes, operate on an assumption of distrust, which creates an antagonistic and authoritarian atmosphere. Students, deprived even of the freedom to go to the bathroom at will, become totally dependent upon authorities for direction, unable to assume any responsibility even if it is offered. They learn from the school that docility and conformity are the best strategies for survival.

Throughout the twentieth century, school reformers, including those of the 1960's, have accomplished remarkably little, Silberman correctly observes. In fact, he is most acute when he analyzes the failures and weaknesses of a number of recent widely proclaimed, but ultimately disappointing, innovations: educational television, the new physics and related curricular reform movements, team teaching, the nongraded classroom, and computer-assisted instruction. The schools at all levels fail: They do not teach skills or produce knowledge in the conventional sense; they reinforce the handicaps of poverty and race; and they try to root out whatever traces of independence and individuality they can find in the personalities of their students. The weaknesses of teacher education, Silberman bluntly but fairly claims, compound all of these problems. Intellectually vapid, inheriting a tradition that neglects questions of purpose, nearly useless in a practical sense, teacher education is a disgrace. Its quality is not helped by snobbish professors of liberal arts who offer their criticisms, but rarely their help, from a safe and jealously guarded distance.

If anyone remains unconvinced that there is a crisis in education and that the schools are failing miserably (and, unfortunately, such people may still be a majority), Silberman's book should shatter his complacency and arouse his indignation. But how are we to account for the awful situation that confronts us, and what are we to do about it? Here, as I have already observed, Silberman unfortunately has much less to offer.

He has a straightforward view of the cause of educational failure: "What is mostly wrong with the public schools is due not to venality or indifference or stupidity, but to mindlessness" (p. 10). "Mindlessness" he defines as "the failure or refusal to think seriously about educational purpose, the reluctance to question established practice" (p. 11). According to Silberman, mindlessness pervades American society, accounting not only for its bad schools but for other major social difficulties as well. We have simply been too preoccupied, too lazy, or too self-interested to think seriously and reflectively about the purposes of our activities and institutions. The lack of correspondence between the complexity of the problems Silberman describes and the reasons he gives for their continued existence is startling. To attribute the persistent failure of a major social institution to a 125-year fit of mindlessness appears almost tongue-in-cheek from an observer so acute, informed, and intelligent as Charles Silberman.

However, his explanation has two functions, positive or negative, depending on one's point of view. First of all, it removes the hint of personal threat implicit in at least most social criticism. No one in particular is at fault for what has happened. We can all—educationist, parent, citizen—be comfortable in the knowledge that our motives and our intentions have not been blameworthy. Mr. Silberman is not attacking us; despite his portrait of our failure, he is really doing little more than giving us a strong exhortation to pull up our socks.

Second, and more serious, attributing educational failure to mindlessness removes the blame not only from individuals but from the larger social and economic system in which schools operate. Unlike the educational radicals whom he criticizes, Silberman does not even hint, to paraphrase Paul Goodman, that the problem of education is that young people do not have a worthy society in which to grow up. There is no question, in Silberman's view, that schools can be made well without a major overhaul of the structures that surround and sustain them. It is not the requirements of industrial capitalism, the obsession with law and order on the cheap, or the persistence of class bias and racism that have produced educational disaster. It is simply mindlessness.

It would be comforting to believe that Silberman is right, but unfortunately, as this book has shown, it would be difficult for anyone reasonably versed in the history and sociology of education to accept his explanation. Educational inequalities have not resulted from mindlessness. They have been quite deliberate. The inequality in the educational system, it is not unfair to say, is a reflex of the inequality in the social structure. Schools are now, and they have always been, reflections of class structure, which they have reinforced rather than altered. Thus, it was no accident or example of simple mindlessness when a white teacher told Malcolm X that he had better give up his hope of becoming a lawyer and be a carpenter instead. That, in fact, is the message that public schools have been designed to give the average lower-class boy, black or white.

The same sort of explanation must be offered for Silberman's second major indictment of the schools: their emphasis on docility. Here, the case is crystal clear, because, as we have observed, it can be made from explicit statements in educational documents spanning a period from early in the nineteenth century until the present. People urged the introduction of systems of public education, including compulsory schooling, to socialize the poor. Throughout American history educational promoters have argued quite explicitly that the purposes of schooling should be more moral than intellectual; the formation of attitudes, that is to say, has been of far greater importance than the development of intellectual or cognitive skills.

Silberman is quite wrong to imply that little thought has been given to educational purpose. School reformers have always considered the relation of the details of curriculum, pedagogy, and structure to larger social and educational objectives. The problem is that those objectives have usually stressed the inculcation of the virtues that, it has been thought, would ensure law, order, and productivity at the lowest possible cost: restraint, reliability, punctuality, and docility.

Silberman feels that the balance in American education has tipped too far toward the cognitive. On the basis of the evidence he presents—the preoccupation with order, control, and conformity at the core of the school experience—as well as on the basis of the historical record, it is not easy to accept that conclusion. It would be more appropriate to say, as I have tried to argue, that schools have been so deeply concerned with the affective, so committed to the primacy of attitude over intellect, that they have never paid sufficiently serious attention to cognitive skills, or to knowledge. Silberman's arguments, consequently, do not offer a new direction for American education. His stress on the need to emphasize the affective is a continuation of a very old tradition. The problem with that tradition, most starkly, is that poor people do not need another lesson in how to behave, even if that behavior is to be liberated rather than repressed. They need the knowledge and skills to move out of poverty. Affective schooling could become a particularly subtle form of "repressive desublimation," to use Marcuse's term. It could be a distraction rather than a benefit to people whose long-term interests would best be served by the redistribution of power and income. In this way, affective education without too much difficulty could serve the purposes of social control for which traditional repressive schools have suddenly become inadequate.

I do not care to question the desirability of informal education modeled on English infant schools, which Silberman advocates; I am willing, for the sake of argument, to grant its superiority to what goes on in the average American classroom. But I do wish to ask, again, about its larger purposes. What can we expect from the widespread introduction of informal education into American schools? Silberman discusses British schools in a fashion similar to the way he discusses American ones: in a social vacuum. He nowhere probes the connections between the schools and the social order in an attempt to find out if informal education is making any difference to the quality of British life. Nor do we learn from him precisely what the connection is between educational and social improvement. In fact, as he admits early in his book, since World War II there has been a phenomenal increase in educational achievements within America. Americans are a

more educated, more thoroughly schooled people than ever
before. Yet few people would claim to discern much connection between that fact and any improvement in the quality
or justice of American life.

Silberman's optimistic prediction that meaningful educational change can occur within existing school systems over-
looks the connection between the structure of those systems
and the educational outcomes that he deplores. However,
two related features of those school systems have important
consequences for the sort of learning that can go on within
them and the objectives that they can reach; those features
are their control (the powerlessness of the people whom they
serve) and their form (bureaucracy). We often think of
bureaucracy, or any other organizational form, as a disem-
bodied, somewhat neutral shell. In fact, organizational form,
as the history of bureaucracy in this book reveals, reflects social values and social purposes, and the structure and control
of education cannot be divorced from what happens within
classrooms. That should be clear from their history and from
each of the historical accounts discussed in this Epilogue.
Introducing informal education into public educational systems without making other radical alterations will be—as
was, for example, the project method—like moving around the
furniture in a box. It is the walls of the box itself that must
be torn down if education is to serve new purposes.

The argument that structural reform must precede a change
in educational purpose and function raises the issue of community control. *Crisis in the Classroom* contains a long chapter on educational reform movements in the 1960's. That
chapter does not mention the movement for community control or decentralization. Neither topic, strange to say, is mentioned elsewhere in the book. Yet, to many people surely,
these movements are where the action is in school reform.
One can only conclude that Silberman is committed to the
existing structure of public education. The voucher system,

performance contracting, radical decentralization—these are not the kinds of reforms he advocates or even cares to discuss. So far as one might gather from *Crisis in the Classroom*, the crisis at Ocean Hill–Brownsville never occurred. Anyone previously unaware of proposals for changing the control and funding of public education would leave Silberman's book without realizing that intelligent, informed, sane people consider these radical measures to be live options. There are limits beyond which Silberman does not help his reader to go.

In fact, his book rests comfortably within the long-standing style of elite reform that has marked American education since early in the nineteenth century. In America, groups of influential people, considering themselves especially expert, have tried, often with success, to force educational change. Social policy and social change, it is assumed, issue from the top down. The problem is that this style of reform works badly. Innovations introduced in this way have not fared well; somehow, they have not met the goals set by their sponsors, who remain unable to account for their failure. The example *par excellence* is the public school system, founded and developed in precisely this manner. Silberman himself documents its continued failure, but he fails to draw the correct moral, which is this: Elite social and educational reform, like welfare bureaucracy, is bankrupt as social policy. At this point in history, any reform worthy of the name must begin with a redistribution of power and resources. That is the only way in which to change the patterns of control and inaccessible organizational structures that dominate American life. It is the only way in which to make education, and other social institutions as well, serve new purposes.

There is no doubt in my mind that, if we change the schools in the direction Silberman suggests, they will become nicer places for children to be. This alone would be a great improvement. But if that is all we do, we shall fail to make education more equal, to eradicate the class and race biases that inhere in educational structures, or to affect the society that surrounds the school. To move on those fronts requires not only considering solutions that Silberman does not discuss but raising questions that he seems reluctant to ask. Silberman has tamed educational discontent. By co-opting instead of resisting it, he has removed its threat and, unfortunately, its promise. He has shown the comfortable way to educational radicalism; others undoubtedly will follow, happy that they can enlist in the cause of justice without sacrifice.

Curiously, and sadly, radical school reform sometimes suffers the same weakness as *Crisis in the Classroom*. For neither rests firmly on any political philosophy or any clear conception of the relationship between education and social change. Two fine, recent, and radical books make this conclusion unavoidable. One is Jonathan Kozol's *Free Schools*, the other Allen Graubard's brilliant *Free the Children*, the best book on contemporary education that I have read. Too often, Graubard shows, the isolated, scattered instances of radical school reform remain primarily attempts to make education pleasant for small groups of children. Radicals either avoid the relation of their pedagogical theory to the social role of education or make the traditional, unwarranted American assumption about the power of a right education to cure a sick society. Indeed, an intellectual softness often undercuts the potential effectiveness of radical educational theory. For naive and untenable assumptions about the nature and role of freedom and an unresolved ambivalence to authority sometimes vitiate the effectiveness of libertarian pedagogical rhetoric by ignoring the restraints and warnings offered by John Dewey decades ago.

Though deeply sympathetic to free schools, radical politics, and a more libertarian pedagogy, Kozol and Graubard both underscore the class bias of much contemporary educational radicalism. A denigration of disciplined intellect, an exaltation of emotions, an emphasis on manual rather than cognitive skills may be useful for anxious, repressed upper-middle-class children. But the needs of the poor, white and black, are very different, as their parents well know. Kozol writes that

> . . . even the most highly 'conscious' and politically sophisticated parents of poor children in such cities as my own draw back in hesitation, fear or anger at the often condescending, if in the long run idealistic, statements and intentions of those who attempt to tell them to forget about English syntax and the preparation for the Mathematics College Boards but send away for bean seeds and for organic food supplies and get into 'group-talk' and 'encounter.' It seems to me that the parents are less backward and more realistic than some of their white co-workers are prepared to recognize . . . a tough, aggressive, skeptical and inventive 'skill' like learning how to undermine and to attack a tough and racist and immensely diffcult examination for the civil service, for City College or for Harvard Law School rings a good deal more of deep-down revolution than the handlooms and the science gadgets and the gerbil cages that have come . . . to constitute an innovative orthodoxy on a scale no less totalitarian than the old Scott, Foresman reader [p. 32].

Kozol and Graubard make unmistakable the connection between politics and pedagogy. By implication they unhappily reveal that the radical school movement of today offers little more promise of altering the relations between school and society than Charles Silberman. A workable, intellectually sound, and politically radical program of educational reform continues to elude the American left; in education as in politics, the left continues to concede victory in a contest it is unprepared to enter.

A Note on Sources,
Personal and Otherwise

The sources of this book are people as well as historical documents. I have talked and argued with, shown drafts to, tried ideas on, and received insights from, more people than I could possibly list. But I would like to mention a few of them by name. David Tyack read and argued with me about the chapter on Boston before it was published in its longer form; as well, our conversations throughout the last few years about urban education and his own research into the late nineteenth and early twentieth centuries have been extremely helpful. Similarly, my conversations with Clarence Karier and his own revisionist ideas about Dewey came at precisely the time when I needed help in putting together progressive educational thought and municipal reform. In the last few years I have also benefited greatly from Charles Bidwell's criticisms of my work. As in my earlier work, Dan Calhoun played an important role in this book, perhaps more important than he realizes: first by pointing me toward Lynn Marshall's "The Strange Stillbirth of the Whig Party" (*American Historical*

195

Review, 72 January, 1967); later by asking exactly the right question about an early draft of an essay on alternative models. During the last several years Stephan Thernstrom, too, has offered enormous encouragement and intelligent criticism.

As much as anyone, my students have contributed to the development of my ideas over the past five years. For their good and critical conversation on matters related directly to this book, I would especially like to thank Barbara Brenzel, Susan Houston, Gordon McLennan, Alison Prentice, and Peter Ross. During the summer of 1970 the students in my course on contemporary controversy in urban education contributed to the last chapter of this book by their refusal to let me get away easily with my arguments. The contributions of my wife, Edda, are very special; without her I am sure this book would still be undone.

This book is addressed to the "general reader," a person I have yet to meet but in whose existence publishers (and who am I to doubt them?) fervently believe. Consequently, I have dispensed throughout with the apparatus of scholarship. I refer readers who would like citations to a number of my previous writings, which document most of the material in this book: "From Voluntarism to Bureaucracy in American Education," *Sociology of Education* (Summer, 1971), a slightly different version of Chapter One; "The Emergence of Bureaucracy in Urban Education: The Boston Case, 1850–1884," *History of Education Quarterly,* two parts (Summer, 1968; Fall, 1968), a much more detailed account of the events recounted in Chapter Two; "The New Departure in Quincy, 1875–1881: The Nature of Nineteenth-Century Educational Reform," *New England Quarterly* (March, 1967), a close examination of Quincy under Francis Parker. *The Irony of Early School Reform: Educational Innovation in Mid-Nineteenth-Century Massachusetts* (Cambridge: Harvard University Press, 1968, reprinted by Beacon Press, 1970) contains documentation on points made throughout this discussion. And, finally, *School*

Reform: Past and Present (Boston: Little, Brown, 1971) is a book of readings where many of the documents that have influenced me most may be found.

Two writers more than any others have influenced my interpretation of contemporary social and cultural concerns. They are Theodore Roszak, through his brilliant book *The Making of the Counter-Culture* (Garden City: Doubleday, 1969), and Paul Goodman, who remains for me the wisest, most humane, and most insightful of contemporary social critics.

This is not the place for a detailed bibliographic discussion of American educational history. But some especially important books should be mentioned for the reader who wishes to pursue further some of the matters discussed in these pages. There is no adequate history of American education, no text or general survey to which I can with confidence refer the reader. *The Educating of Americans: A Documentary History* (Boston: Houghton-Mifflin, 1969), edited by Daniel Calhoun, is by far the best book of its kind, an original, insightful, and fascinating collection. Likewise, David Tyack's book of readings, *Turning Points in American Educational History* (Waltham, Mass.: Blaisdell, 1967), contains a great many useful documents, imaginatively arranged. Clarence Karier's *Man, Society and Education: A History of American Educational Ideas* (Chicago: Scott, Foresman, 1967), is a very fine over-all discussion of educational thought. Provocative and useful, too, is Rush Welter, *Popular Education and Democratic Thought in America* (New York: Columbia University Press, 1962).

The seminal essay in the revival of interest in the history of education that began in the 1960's is Bernard Bailyn's *Education in the Forming of American Society* (Chapel Hill: University of North Carolina Press, 1960), a brief excursion in hypothetical history. Although the demographic analysis of English and of Colonial society is proving that much of what Bailyn suggested about the family cannot be sustained by the facts, the essay nevertheless remains a *tour de force* that must be read by anyone who is seriously interested in American education. The most recent and comprehensive discussion of Colonial education is Lawrence Cremin's *American Education: The Colonial Experience* (New York: Harper & Row, 1970), an impressive work of scholarship with an old-fashioned (in the best sense of the term) approach; its bibliography is the most complete available on the subject. There are extremely useful documents on both the Colonial period and the first half of the nineteenth century in Robert H. Bremner, ed., *Children and Youth in America: A Documentary History* (Cambridge: Harvard University Press, 1970).

There is not a great deal written about the first half of the nineteenth century that can be recommended. Certainly, James McLachlan's *American Boarding Schools: A History* (New York: Scribner's, 1970), a splendid survey of the subject, must be included in any list. For the most part, however, the reader will have to go to journal articles; among the most useful are Jonathan Messerli, "Localism and State Control in Horace Mann's Reform of the Common Schools," *American Quarterly*, 17 (Spring, 1965); David Tyack, "The Kingdom of God and the Common School," *Harvard Educational Review*, 36 (Fall, 1966); Timothy Smith, "Protestant Schooling and American Nationality, 1800–1850," *The Journal of American History*, 53 (March, 1967); and Daniel Calhoun, "From Noah Webster to Chauncey Wright: The Intellectual as Prognostic," *Harvard Educational Review*, 36 (Fall, 1966). For books that treat less specialized subjects but provide important interpretive frameworks I recommend Oscar and Mary Handlin, *Commonwealth: A Study of the Role of Government in the American Economy, Massachusetts, 1774–1861* (New York: New York University Press, 1947), and Marvin Myers, *The Jacksonian Persuasion* (Stanford, Calif.: Stanford University Press, 1957). The history of education paralleled the history of prisons, mental hospitals, and reform schools;

reading about other sorts of institutions thus illuminates the subject of schools. The reader who wants to learn about the history of education would therefore do well to examine Gerald Grob's excellent book *The State and the Mentally Ill* (Chapel Hill: University of North Carolina Press, 1966), and Walter D. Lewis, *From Newgate to Dannemora* (Ithaca, N.Y.: Cornell University Press, 1965).

For the progressive period the secondary literature about education is not copious. There is, first, Lawrence Cremin's *The Transformation of the School* (New York: Random House, 1961). Although I disagree with Cremin's interpretation of progressivism, I have great admiration for this book, which is a graceful and learned intellectual history. Raymond Callahan, *Education and the Cult of Efficiency* (Chicago: University of Chicago Press, 1962), contains a great deal of useful data, although I would quarrel with much of his interpretation. Edward Krug, *The Shaping of the American High School* (New York: Harper & Row, 1964), is an indispensable source of information on the development of the high school curriculum. David Tyack's work on the centralization of schools and Clarence Karier's on Dewey and on the testing movement, most of which remains unpublished, are writings that anyone interested in these subjects should watch for with some anticipation.

There is little published material on what went on within schools and within communities during the late nineteenth and early twentieth centuries. The most complete and useful data we have about the twentieth century are to be found in Helen and Robert Merrill Lynd's *Middletown* (New York: Harcourt, Brace, 1929), and *Middletown in Transition* (New York: Harcourt, Brace, 1937). Of the more general books on this period in American history, the one that has impressed and influenced me most is Robert Wiebe, *The Search for Order, 1877–1920* (New York: Hill & Wang, 1967).

Moving closer to the present, the problem one finds is an embarrassment of riches. Books on educational reform seem to come out almost daily; I have long stopped trying to keep up with them. Of those I have read I have found the following most useful: Paul Goodman's *Growing Up Absurd* (New York: Random House, 1956), *Compulsory Mis-education* (New York: Horizon, 1964), and *The New Reformation* (New York: Random House, 1970) stand out as works of social and educational criticism. The mood of disenchanted students is captured well in Tom Seligson and Marc Libarle, eds., *The High School Revolutionaries* (New York: Random House, 1970). Henry Resnik, in *Turning on the System* (New York: Pantheon Books, Random House, 1970), offers a lucid and insightful history of a very recent movement of educational reform, a history depressingly easy to predict on the basis of past experience. Maurice Berube and Marilyn Gittell, in *Confrontation at Ocean-Hill Brownsville* (New York: Praeger, 1969), have provided a clear (as much as that subject can be) and intelligent book of readings representing a wide variety of points of view. Similarly, Ronald and Beatrice Gross, in *Radical School Reform* (New York: Simon & Schuster, 1970), have compiled a very useful anthology of contemporary viewpoints.

The history of Negro education remains, appallingly, unwritten. Henry Bullock has written a sometimes questionable survey in *A History of Negro Education in the South from 1619 to the Present* (Cambridge: Harvard University Press, 1967; paperback New York: Praeger, 1970). Louis Harlan's *Separate and Unequal: Public School Campaigns and Racism in the Southern Seaboard States, 1901–1915* (Chapel Hill: University of North Carolina Press, 1958) remains a more incisive and very useful source on Southern developments after the Civil War. Herbert Gutman's forthcoming book on the Reconstruction period promises to put the whole subject in a new perspective. On the point of view of black intellectuals, August Meir, *Negro Thought in America, 1880–1915*

(Ann Arbor: University of Michigan Press, 1963), is quite helpful.

Educators of every period have left documents that reveal their thought and their activities. Most school districts have records that enable one to reconstruct quite precisely what happened there. From school reports, censuses, and other sources it is possible to cull surprisingly large amounts of information about school attendance, school finances, teachers, and related subjects. Except for the writings of the most famous of educators, these sources have scarcely been tapped. That accounts for the massive ignorance about what happened and why it still persists concerning educational history, as I have mentioned throughout these pages. For anyone seriously interested in making more decisive our knowledge about how American education came to be, or in just finding out for himself, the material is at hand.

Addendum: August, 1974

A number of works that have appeared since this note on sources first was written should be mentioned. In the text I have discussed some of these already: Carl Kaestle, *The Evolution of an Urban School System: New York City, 1750–1850* (Cambridge: Harvard University Press, 1973), is the best account available of the origins of a big-city school system. Stanley K. Schultz, *The Culture Factory: Boston Public Schools, 1789–1860* (New York: Oxford University Press, 1973), is a useful account of developments in Boston. Marvin Lazerson, *Origins of the Urban School: Public Education in Massachusetts 1870–1915* (Cambridge: Harvard University Press, 1971), provides a fine analysis of the origins of major innovations, and David B. Tyack, *The One Best Sys-*

tem (Cambridge: Harvard University Press, 1974), examines the problem of organization and control and provides an excellent overview of the history of urban schooling; Tyack's book also has a full and exceptionally useful bibliography. Clarence J. Karier, Paul Violas, and Joel Spring, *Roots of Crisis: American Education in the Twentieth Century* (Chicago: Rand McNally, 1973), provocatively connects educational reform with the history of American liberalism and the revisionist interpretation of modern American history. Charles Silberman, *Crisis in the Classroom* (New York: Random House, 1970), is the best example of the connection between liberalism and educational reform today, while Jonathan Kozol, *Free Schools* (Boston: Houghton Mifflin, 1972), and Allen Graubard, *Free the Children* (New York: Pantheon, 1972), provide exceptionally intelligent commentaries on the contemporary radical reform movement in education.

Also useful on the origins of public education is Jonathan Messerli, *Horace Mann: A Biography* (New York: Knopf, 1972). On later developments two revisionist works are Joel H. Spring, *Education and the Rise of the Corporate State* (Boston: Beacon Press, 1972), and a rather shrill and distorted book by Colin Greer, *The Great School Legend: A Revisionist Interpretation of American Public Education* (New York: Basic Books, 1972), Daniel Calhoun, *The Intelligence of a People* (Princeton: Princeton University Press, 1973), brilliantly relates educational developments to the history of American culture. A collection of articles illustrating recent educational historiography and arranged as a text is Michael B. Katz, ed., *Education in American History: Readings on the Social Issues* (New York: Praeger, 1973).

The history of women and the history of the family are areas of special interest to historians of education. In the past few years some important work in these fields has finally begun to appear. See, for example, the special issue on "Reinterpreting Women's Education" of the *History of Education Quarterly*, Vol. 14, No. 1 (Spring, 1974); Michael Gordon, ed., *The American Family in Social-Historical Perspective* (New York: St. Martin's, 1973), an exceptionally intelligent and useful collection; and Theodore K. Rabb and Robert I. Rotberg, eds., *The Family in History: Interdisciplinary Essays* (New York: Harper Torchbooks, 1973).

Finally, readers should take note of two excellent and recent collections of documents that bear quite directly on the material in this book, both in the Teachers College Classics in Education Series. One is Carl F. Kaestle, ed., *Joseph Lancaster and the Monitorial School Movement* (1973); the other is Marvin Lazerson and W. Norton Grubb, eds., *American Education and Vocationalism: A Documentary History* (1974).

Index